UNDERSTA.
BOUNDARIE. AND
CONTAINMENT IN
CLINICAL PRACTICE

The Society of Analytical Psychology Monograph Series
Hazel Robinson (Series Editor)
Published and distributed by Karnac Books

Other titles in the SAP Monograph Series

Understanding Narcissism in Clinical Practice
   Hazel Robinson & Victoria Graham Fuller

Understanding Perversion in Clinical Practice:
Structure and Strategy in the Psyche
   Fiona Ross

Understanding the Self–Ego Relationship in Clinical Practice:
Towards Individuation
   Margaret Clark

UNDERSTANDING BOUNDARIES AND CONTAINMENT IN CLINICAL PRACTICE

*Rebecca Brown and
Karen Stobart*

LONDON AND NEW YORK

First published 2008 by Karnac Books Ltd.

Published 2018 by Routledge
2 Park Square, Milton Park, Abingdon, Oxon OX14 4RN
711 Third Avenue, New York, NY 10017, USA

*Routledge is an imprint of the Taylor & Francis Group, an
informa business*

British Library Cataloguing in Publication Data

A C.I.P. records for this book is available from the British Library.

ISBN 9781855753938 (pbk)

Edited, designed and produced by The Studio Publishing
Services Ltd
www.publishingservicesuk.co.uk
e-mail: studio@publishingservicesuk.co.uk

Contents

Contents

About the Authors

Rebecca Brown is a Training Analyst with the Society of Analytical Psychology and also supervises for the British Association of Psychotherapists and the London Centre for Psychotherapy. She is a former Chair of the Society and has been involved for many years in its analytic training programme. She is also involved in running a public programme for counsellors and psychotherapists in Oxford. Her background is in counselling, psychiatric social work, and psychotherapy.

Karen Stobart is a Professional Member of the Society of Analytical Psychology, working in private practice in London and in the National Health Service as a Consultant Psychotherapist (Adult).

Preface to the Series

This series of clinical practice monographs is being produced primarily for the benefit of trainees on psychotherapy and psychodynamic counselling courses. The authors are Jungian analysts who have trained at the Society of Analytical Psychology, with extensive experience of teaching both theory and practice.

The rationale for this series is in part to do with the expensive and time-consuming task of accessing all the pertinent books and papers for any one clinical subject. These single-issue monographs have been kept relatively brief and cannot claim to be comprehensive, but we hope that each volume brings together some of the major theorists and their ideas in a comprehensible way, including references to significant and interesting texts.

Much of the literature provided for students of psychotherapy has been generated from four or five-times weekly analytic work, which can be confusing for students whose psychodynamic courses may be structured on the basis of less frequent sessions. The authors of these monographs have aimed to hold this difference in mind. In the Introducton and elsewhere, their use of terminology is explored. We have borrowed gratefully from the work of our supervisees in many settings, and we are above all indebted to our patients. Where a patient's material is recognizable, their permission to publish has been given. In other cases, we have amalgamated and disguised clinical material to preserve anonymity.

When a training is 'eclectic', that is, offering several different psychodynamic perspectives, a particular difficulty can arise with integration – or rather *non*-integration of psychoanalytic and Jungian analytic ideas. The teaching on such trainings is often presented in blocks: a term devoted to 'Freud', another to 'Jung', and so on. It is frequently the students who are left with the job of trying to see where these do and do not fit together, and this can be a daunting, even depressing, experience. SAP analysts are in a better position than most to offer some help here, because its members have been working on this integration since the organization was founded in 1936 (incorporated in 1946). Although retaining a strong relationship with 'Zurich' or 'Classical' Jungian scholarship, SAP members have evolved equally strong links with psychoanalysis. Recent years have brought a number of joint conferences to supplement the many 'cross-party' alliances.

Any patient, but particularly a trainee, will naturally tend to adopt the language of his or her therapist when talking about their work. Those readers who are unfamiliar with Jungian terms may wish to consult the *Critical Dictionary of Jungian Analysis* (Samuels, Shorter & Plaut, 1986), while those unfamiliar with psychoanalytic terms may turn to *The Language of Psychoanalysis* (Laplanche & Pontalis, 1988). But all patients are united by their human suffering far more than they are divided by language. Just as people from non-western cultures have to make what they can of their western-trained psychotherapists, so each patient–therapist pair eventually evolves a unique way of understanding their joint experiences in the consulting-room. It is our view that each stream of psychotherapy has strengths and weaknesses, and the wise trainee will take the best bits from each. We hope that this series may help a little with the psychodynamic 'Tower of Babel'.

We want to thank Karnac for their patience and help in bringing the series to publication. Our intention is to gradually add further volumes on some of the principal clinical issues. I therefore want to end by thanking my colleagues within the SAP for their work so far – and for their work to come.

Hazel Robinson
Series Editor

Introduction

We propose to investigate the meaning and purpose of boundaries within and around the therapeutic experience. The term boundary is borrowed from geography; as in geography, boundaries can function as barriers or delineators. They can 'keep in' or 'keep out'; they can hinder or enable safe passage from one place to another. A boundary is more than a simple line delineating one space from another; it is an entity with properties that demand a response if they are to be negotiated.

Boundaries circumscribe a space that can be viewed objectively, or experienced subjectively, as a 'container'. For the uninitiated, this therapeutic container can be difficult to penetrate. Even health professionals such as GPs and psychiatrists often do not know how to access psychotherapy organizations and their referral networks. Also, real constraints on the availability of counselling and psychotherapy within the National Health Service, and the cost of private sector services, may prohibit access to the help being sought.

Chapter One, 'Why Boundaries?', addresses the gradual evolution of therapeutic boundaries in psychodynamic work. Freud's understanding of the power of the transference led him to develop guidelines for the treatment of psychoanalytic patients (Freud, 1912b). Jung expanded this into an understanding of the effect a patient may have upon the therapist, known as countertransference. In science, the conditions in which any experiment is conducted are kept as stable and constant as possible; the inter-reacting chemicals are protected from possible contamination from without while being themselves confined within a container. These conditions and procedures are necessary in order to determine the meaning of the observed interaction. Of course, in therapy we are dealing with the living and largely unknowable material of the human mind, but the value of the container is similar.

The safety provided by reliability, regularity, confidentiality, etc. allow the client to express aspects of his past and present experience usually felt to be too painful or shameful to be shared with others. This can result in a relationship of intimate trust in, and sometimes dependence on, the therapist. Significant childhood experiences are often re-experienced and understood for the first time. Chapter Two offers a brief exploration of boundary development in infancy and childhood and shows how aspects of this development can be expressed years later in the consulting room.

The intimate therapeutic encounter is defined by practical constraints that differentiate therapeutic 'space' from the outside world. Chapter Three explores issues such as money and time. Patients who place themselves in such a vulnerable position are protected in part by an individual therapist's professional sense of self. Chapter Four describes the central importance of the containing function of the psychotherapist's mind, constructed through training and personal therapy or analysis. Chapter Five describes how therapeutic work can be affected by the setting in which it is taking place. These issues will be explored in depth throughout by the use of clinical examples.

The use of clinical material by the authors immediately raises the issue of confidentiality, explored in depth in Chapter Six. It is difficult to balance the need to illustrate what actually happens in therapy with the need to protect the confidentiality of the relationship. We have decided to use fictitious examples based on the factual experience of our and others' work.

Chapter Seven explores some of the issues involved in the professional boundaries that surround the practising psychotherapist. This includes the Codes of Ethics and good practice of the training organizations, and legislation relevant to clinical work. Chapter Eight, which explores issues to do with endings, brings the book to a close.

About terminology

In this monograph we are addressing our remarks to counsellors, psychotherapists, psychiatrists, trainees of these professions and indeed any other mental health practitioners, who are working with people at an intensity of one or two sessions per week. Naturally, some of what we say may also be applicable to more intensive forms of intervention such as psychoanalytic psychotherapy or analysis, but these are beyond the scope of this book except for the remarks about referring patients. Although there are areas of overlap between psychotherapy and analysis, (particularly for psychotherapists who themselves may have been in analysis), there are also important differences in the use of transference/countertransference interpretations and in the approach to unconscious material.

The terms 'counsellor', 'therapist', and 'psychotherapist' are problematic. Ten or more years ago, each term would have had a less ambiguous meaning. The past decade has brought much muddying of the waters and the terms are now often used interchangeably and in our opinion loosely, if not incorrectly. Although some aspects of the therapeutic work of counsellors and psycho-therapists do overlap or at times form a continuum, there remain important differences between the two professions that we do not wish to ignore. The picture is complicated by the fact that some experienced counsellors, particularly those doing longer-term work, might work in a way closer to what would ordinarily be termed psychotherapy, while other mental health professionals who use the term psychotherapy are working in a way closer to what most people would call counselling! When there are aspects of the work that pertain to both counsellor and psycho-therapist, we will use the terms 'therapeutic work' or 'practitioner', or 'counsellor and psychotherapist'. Otherwise, we will refer to these professions separately. The clinical examples will use the designation of the original worker.

Equally, we are not using the terms 'psychotherapist' and 'psychotherapy' in the all-inclusive sense that they are often used today to include the whole range of psycho-therapeutic work and mental health workers. We think this can be confusing both to the public and to the profes-sionals' own understanding of who they are and what they do. While there are many different professionals who can offer treatment to the patient, their titles are presently different and the nature of what they do can be different. A rather dull but better all-inclusive term for the wide range of practitioners working in the field would be 'mental health practitioners'. Such a term acknowledges the range of therapeutic workers who work with mental health problems, but does not 'paper over' the differences between them.

The terms 'client' and 'patient' are again words that have had clearer boundaries in the past. Traditionally, counsellors tended to refer to 'clients', whereas psychotherapists tended to use the designation 'patients' – particularly in a hospital or institutional setting. More recently, some psychotherapists have preferred to use the term 'client' because of its more ordinary, less medical connotation. In some instances, we have used the word 'client' in order to help differentiate between this form of intervention and the more intensive forms such as psychoanalytic psychotherapy and analysis. In the clinical examples we use the actual designation of the person being treated.

Finally, we have decided to use the pronouns 'he' and 'she' interchangeably and inclusively. As both the client/ patient and the counsellor/psychotherapist may be either male or female, the terms 'he' and 'she' will, in the context of therapeutic work, mean *either 'he' or 'she'*. The more politically correct terminology of 's/he' or 'he and she' tends to become cumbersome especially when used repeatedly.

CHAPTER ONE

WHY BOUNDARIES?

Why are boundaries, and the processes of containment, considered so important to psychodynamic work? Why set aside the same room and the same hour each week for counselling or psychotherapy? Why do the sessions last for a particular length of time? Why are we so careful about giving ample notice of holiday breaks? Those unfamiliar with the work might exclaim, 'Surely clients can cope with some irregularity!' In fact, might it not be better, as the wider culture and the media so often tell us, *not* to encourage too much dependency in this way, particularly in focused, shorter-term work? This chapter explores some of the thinking and assumptions behind these patterns.

Initially, Freud conducted his investigations much as a medical doctor. For example, in the case of Frau Emmy von N, he 'ordered her to be given warm baths and I shall massage her whole body twice a day' (Freud & Breuer, 1895d, p. 50). A brilliant theoretician and clinician, Freud gradually began to analyse the psychological constructions that underpinned such physical treatments. In particular he elucidated the importance of the transference; i.e., the unconscious relationship between patient and clinician. For example, in the case history of 'Dora' Freud wrote,

> If the theory of analytic technique is gone into, it becomes evident that transference is an inevitable necessity ... Transference is the one thing the presence of

1

> which has to be detected almost without assistance and
> with only the slightest clues to go upon, while at the same
> time the risk of making arbitrary inferences has to be
> avoided. [Freud, 1905e, p. 116]

He was developing an understanding of the need for, and
value of, boundaries between analyst and patient. The
difficulties encountered in maintaining such boundaries
became clearer as the emotional effect of the patient upon
the analyst was understood. This is termed the countertransference and Jung was one of the first of the early
followers of Freud to understand the importance of the
concept and its implications for practice.

Jung identified a powerful process, which he described
as '*participation mystique*', in which both patient and
analyst could become unconsciously merged (Jung, 1953,
par. 253). Jung understood its dangers, but the underlying
psychological mechanism was not really understood until
Klein identified the process of projective identification
(Klein, 1946, p. 8). She explored how the infant deals
with early anxieties by projecting them into the mother
and realized that the infant may then identify the mother
with the unpleasant feelings that have been evacuated by
projection; hence the term projective identification.

For a long time, countertransference experiences were
regarded as a hindrance to treatment and to be minimized. Then, the dynamics of projective identification
were further elucidated by analysts such as Bion, who realized the vital developmental role played by the mother's
mind in processing (detoxifying) and making meaningful
the infant's projections (Bion, 1970). Analysts realized
that in a parallel way countertransference could also represent a powerful therapeutic tool. Working with, rather

than trying to dispense with, the countertransference can, however, involve the therapist in complex interpersonal exchanges. In this context, the delineation of, and adherence to, strict professional boundaries has become vital.

A secure and safe container

The process occurring in the therapeutic space needs the protection of both concrete boundaries and the more intangible sense of containment. Almost all psychotherapeutic approaches utilize processes in the work similar to those of maternal containment (although awareness of this might vary). When powerful emotions are being addressed, or are as yet in the background, a secure container for those feelings is important, if not essential. A routine that is familiar provides a safe and reliable setting in which to experience that which is *not* safe and reliable, that which might be new, shaky, or perhaps even explosive.

In chemistry the conditions in which an experiment is conducted are kept as stable and constant as possible. In this way, the interacting chemicals are protected from contamination, and the chemist is protected from harm. Jung used images from the work of medieval alchemists to describe the therapeutic encounter. The alchemists chemical experiments, which were attempts to turn dross into gold, were depicted in a series of mystical pictures, the Rosarium Philosophorum (Jung, 1946). Jung likened the therapeutic process to the alchemical container, or 'vas', which is depicted in the Rosarium as a royal bath. One image shows a naked king and queen – patient and therapist – descending into the bath. Their nakedness illustrates the vulnerability of the participants in the therapeutic process. Undressing without undue embarrassment requires the security of a contained, very private, boundaried space. We could say that in therapy the 'chemicals' are the conscious and unconscious thoughts and feelings of the patient and therapist.

Michael Fordham, a Jungian analyst, who worked extensively with children, developed Jung's work on containment:

> . . . the alchemical vessel in which [the alchemists] substances were heated must be firmly closed so that nothing shall escape from it. In the relation between the mother and her baby the mother's containing function is essential; first she contains her baby physically in her womb, then she holds him in her arms and also contains him in her mind and her emotions. Periodically, in an emotional crisis, all she is required to do is to hold her baby whilst he works through an emotional conflict. . . . But the containment is not only physical. In the first place her maternal reverie reflects and digests her infant's state of mind and she can feed back to her baby the result of her mental but non-verbal activity through action and talk. [Fordham, 1985, p. 209]

Highlighting the invisible

In the course of ordinary life, boundaries are broken all the time. The bus is scheduled to arrive at 8.30; invariably it comes later. You have arranged to speak with a colleague in private; more likely than not you are interrupted. Intrusions of one kind or another can happen so frequently that we come to expect them or hardly notice when they do. In our conscious life, you might say we become acclimatized to such changes, but in therapeutic work boundaries and the interactions that take place around them matter in a different way. In creating a safe and reliable frame around the work, the boundaries themselves become the focus of feelings when their containing function 'fails'. Unlike the bus that comes late so often we no longer notice or even expect it to happen, it is the opposite – invariably the sessions *do* start on time so that when they do not, we notice with a heightened sense of perception. Although we do not set out to break boundaries and the containment they provide, when it does happen it can be like putting a magnifying glass to a hitherto invisible part of the psyche. That was one of the reasons for the early emphasis in psychoanalysis on the 'blank screen' of the consulting room. The blank screen highlights what would be missed if the background were more changeable.

The therapeutic encounter aims for a time to keep out an important aspect of ordinary social life, the aspect that says, 'It doesn't matter', or 'in polite circles we don't make a fuss'. In long-term counselling and in most forms of psychotherapy we set out to notice what, on a social level, might be insignificant infringements. It is this aspect of therapy that can be satirized in popular culture, as if those of us engaged in the enterprise are somewhat strange in our preoccupation with sessions starting and ending, holiday breaks, and payment of accounts. The therapeutic dialogue is not like an ordinary conversation in which the 'hiccups' of social interaction are disregarded. Even in the initial assessment, the boundary issues (whether appointments are kept, whether the person arrives on time, whether he can tolerate interventions) might high-light aspects of the patient's personality that he could not tell you about directly.

The work is facilitated by the fact that the boundaries are ordinarily in place and so the impact of a change is heightened. Conditions that promote stability include the fixed times of the sessions and confidentiality. But, however carefully boundaries are maintained, there are times when the unexpected happens: the counsellor is unexpectedly delayed, someone else walks into the room, or there is a misunderstanding about holiday dates. These breaks of the boundary can form bridges to important aspects of the work: boundaries that were broken in child-hood (such as betrayal by an important carer) or issues of distrust in the patient's current life.

Clinical example

The client brings up something new and significant just as the end of the session approaches. The counsellor is tempted to extend the time in order to explore it. But if the client is accustomed to the usual length of his sessions, the timing of his new material is probably not mere chance. Consciously or unconsciously, he might have done this because he could count on the session ending at a particular time and could therefore save himself from getting into more than he could manage; he is relying on an unchanging setting to guard his psychological safety. He wants a small portion of this new 'food' and not a whole plateful!

Illuminating the shadow

Whatever the type of treatment – counselling, psycho-therapy, or analysis – what the person brings into the room are feelings and reactions that he might be facing for the first time in his life and, possibly, communicating to another for the first time. The fact that he is there in the room is indicative that this time he has chosen to face his problems in a different way. The therapy might ultimately involve some relief, but not usually without some discomfort or pain as well.

Those parts of our psyches that are hidden and that we find difficult to face, Jung called 'the shadow'. Boundaries and containment encourage trust, which in turn provides a better situation for the exploration of these difficult shadow areas. This is particularly so because much of what we encounter in the shadow is itself related either to a previous breakdown of trust or to trust not having been established in the first place. In spite of the fact that a client might have come to therapy to get in touch with shadow aspects he is likely to feel some resistance to that exploration. However, regular appointments and knowing about holiday breaks well in advance are a part of the solid path that will make a difficult journey more possible.

Confidentiality

Confidentiality, different from secrecy, is a cornerstone of psychodynamic work. It is rarely absolute: counsellors and therapists usually discuss cases with a supervisor; the counsellor might work in an institutional setting where other members of the team will have access to some information; there are circumstances – for example, child abuse – in which statutory authorities may, of legal necessity, become involved. However, in the ordinary course of the work the assumption is that what goes on in the room is private; it is part of a therapeutic context and not a social one. As far as possible, the organic process that is happening between client and counsellor/therapist needs to stay within the room. The client might, naturally, share some of the content and feelings with friends or family but this is not encouraged because the process can be 'diluted' if the focus of the work in the 'here and now' is shifted outside.

A space for the opposites to come together

The emphasis on the unconscious in psychodynamic work, whether explicit or implicit, carries with it a respect for the unspoken. We try to make sense not only of what is said but also of non-verbal forms of communication that at times contradict the verbal. If we only hear 'directed thought' (rational logic) and not also 'undirected thought' (associative or free-flowing thought), we lose a part of the whole – the 'opposites' that Jung believed only together can make sense of the internal world. The contained space and the attitude towards a contained space help to create the conditions needed for these opposites to come together. The capacity to wait and listen for the opposite to emerge depends on the internal sense of containment that we learn through our training and bring from within ourselves (ultimately, from our own experience of therapy).

Clinical example

An eighteen-year-old girl comes for help to decide whether to keep her baby or have an abortion. At first she expresses her desire to get rid of the baby; she feels it would be better, and knows her mother would want her to do so. But the counsellor notices her holding and rubbing her tummy as she speaks. The girl is surprised when this is remarked upon, and then bursts into sobs of grief about the prospect of losing her precious baby.

If the counsellor had identified with the more conscious and immediate feeling, the girl's less conscious feelings would have been missed. The counsellor's capacity to contain and maintain a thinking space allowed other feelings to emerge. Whatever decision is made eventually, it will have been valuable for the young woman to discover her ambivalence.

Promoting thought through frustration

So far, we have looked at boundaries in relation to their capacity to make the space within them more secure, less threatening, more integrative, and more confidential. There is another aspect of their function that would at first appear to be in contrast to these factors. This concerns the function of frustration. In this sense, the experience of 'coming up against a boundary' can feel harsh or unwelcoming. A regular pattern of times might be secure in the sense that it is consistent, but it might also feel withholding or unyielding. Given that there is enough of a working alliance established, this experience of frustration can eventually lead to the development of insight.

Clinical example

A patient found the rigid session times made him feel intolerable rage toward his kindly therapist. He could not express what was, to him, a shameful feeling, but was disheartened because his therapy was going round and round in circles: 'just going over the same old things'. The therapist did not give up. She sensitively contained the patient's frustration until one day he mentioned that he had been a 'Truby King baby': fed at very regular and prescribed times that did not coincide with his hunger. The obvious, but until then unconscious, link was made, and the patient 'let go' his rage with great relief.

The therapist's need for containment

The emphasis thus far has been on the client and how boundaries and containment affect his experience of counselling or therapy. However, the boundaries around the work have an impact on both participants. The counsellor or therapist, although he comes to the session with the greater experience, faces this particular client on this particular day for the first time. In order to explore the unknown, the practitioner also needs the containment of a boundaried space that is not interrupted, that happens at regular intervals, and that has anticipated breaks. The boundaries around the space help the therapist to feel contained, so that he in turn becomes part of the containing space around the client.

A warm, comfortable, quiet, and uninterrupted space, and the boundaries that maintain this, are a vital protection for the therapist's capacity to keep his mind available for the therapeutic encounter. We are only too aware of how fragile a particular state of mind can be, how vulnerable a train of thought is to distraction, noise, or interruption. There are times when a client himself might not notice a boundary being out of place, but if the impingement affects the therapist's ability to function in a containing manner, the client might notice or be affected by a change in the therapist's demeanour.

Acting out

Boundaries serve another protective function and that is in relation to the potential for strong emotions to be acted out. Boundaries remind both participants that, although highly intimate and personal, the therapeutic encounter must not include violence, social contact, or sexual behaviour. For example, at times it can be difficult for the client to distinguish between adult sexual feelings and powerful infantile attachment to a parent. If the therapist does not have adequate supervision for this difficult work, and especially if it touches too closely on his own personal unresolved issues, the feelings might be acted upon.

Jung's understanding of the potential for the therapeutic process to affect and transform both participants led him to emphasize the necessity for the practitioner's own personal therapy. Adequate supervision and personal therapy are a part of the safety net that helps the therapist to contain the material in the session and to continue to understand it symbolically.

Summary

We began this chapter by asking why boundaries are important to the therapeutic process. They create a safe and secure container for the work. They help to illuminate what Jung termed 'the shadow' – our unknown side.

They help to highlight what might otherwise be difficult to see unless it is thrown into relief and magnified. They facilitate confidentiality and trust. They encourage 'the opposites' to emerge. They promote thought and enhanced ego-functioning through an increasing ability to tolerate frustration. They contribute to a necessary sense of security for the practitioner who in turn can be more containing for the patient. They are, finally, a protection for both patient and therapist against acting out.

CHAPTER TWO

BOUNDARY AND CONTAINMENT IN CHILD DEVELOPMENT

Prenatal experience

The very beginnings of life take place in a confined space with clear boundaries. For the first nine months of life the mother's womb is the container that defines the space in which development takes place. This space is defined physically by the walls of the amniotic sac and the womb. It is defined emotionally before, during, and after conception by the hopes and expectations of the parents. At times it is even defined by a lack of hope and expectation. If the father is absent, or even unknown, the space in which the earliest development takes place is still shaped by that fact, by what the mother imagined or hoped the father to be and perhaps by what her experience of her own father and mother was. So, at a time long after their deaths, the grandparents and their parents can still play a part in defining that first space in which the embryo is conceived. In Jungian terms, the collective unconscious has 'collected' around the conception, thus affecting the emotional climate into which the baby is born nine months later.

This first space, then, has both a physical and an emotional boundary. Modern infant research is refining our understanding of how the child might experience this earliest container, the womb. It is certainly not the quiet place we had once thought, for the infant experiences a fair amount of noise from the mother's internal organs. We now know he might even hear noise originating from outside the mother's body. He might find his thumb. He is affected by the mother's emotional state as reflected in her hormones and in turn from their effect on such things as the blood supply to the uterus. He is affected by what she puts into her body (food, drugs, nicotine), by what she might or might not be able to secure for herself (support or love) and even by what is put into the larger container of the room, house, or wider environment in which she lives (the smoke and pollutants of others, both actual and metaphorical). A recent study found a correlation between the food a mother eats during pregnancy and the food a child prefers later on (Mennella, 2005). There is also the question of who else shares in that wider container with the mother and how their interactions affect the emotional space that she and the growing foetus inhabit. In this chapter we shall be considering some of the individual's early experiences of boundary and containment and how these can affect what might be brought years later into the consulting room. It is interesting how a pregnancy that is not wanted can affect the child to such an extent that in therapy years later he might have strong feelings about being seen.

Neonatal experience

In utero and in the very first moments of life outside the womb, the skin functions as a boundary between the baby's inside and his outside, between mother and baby.

Karpf, in a recent article went as far as to describe the skin as 'the perimeter of the self, our rim, our envelope, the point where our insides become outsides, the personal becomes the social'. She further explains that 'the cells which go to make up the central nervous system are the same ones which form the skin, and they develop in the embryo at the same time' (Karpf, 1999, p. 7). It is perhaps not accidental that we sometimes use the terms 'thick- or thin-skinned' to denote the capacity to protect ourselves in relation to another person, to indicate the importance of this earliest of boundaries. It is well recognized that some-one coming into counselling or psychotherapy will need to have developed some kind of defensive structure (or we could say 'skin') to be able to cope with the demands of exposing himself, and particularly so in the more intensive forms of the therapeutic work. Quite often, the initial stages of the work will be focused on helping the individ-ual develop just such resources so as to be able to survive the very experience he is embarking on. The boundaries and sense of containment that we create around the thera-peutic experience could be seen as contributing to or adding another layer of this protective 'skin'.

Michael Fordham's work on infancy postulates a 'primary self' that, even in the earliest days of life, directs an active encounter between baby and the outside world (Fordham, 1985). Once born, there is a space 'between' that is affected by both mother and baby and, of course, by others in that environment. The baby is both contained (or not) in a physical and emotional holding space and at the same time is a part of that containment between himself and his mother.

The experience of the space between mother and baby will be very different depending on the personalities involved and on who else shares that space. The first baby with a full-time mother might be protected from early separation and intrusion or could be submerged into the undiluted impact of her emotions. That same child coming into an established family with several siblings, so close there is little space of his own or so distant there is little contact between children, has a very different experience. The variations are infinite – one or two parents, a step-parent, a grandparent, a same-sex partner or close friend – all have some impact, even if only indirect, through the mother's attitude and experience of them, on the space the baby inhabits.

Clinical example

A client who is an only child with an absent father comes into counselling oblivious to other clients – just as if he were still 'on his own'. His apparent insensitivity to the starting and ending times of the sessions seems to demonstrate an unchallenged assumption that there is simply no one else around. It is as if all the space belongs to him and his mother (or, in the transference, that part of the counsellor whom he expects to share his perception). Not only does he not 'see' the evidence of other clients/siblings, he also cannot 'hear' his counsellor's attempts to draw his attention to the beginning and ending boundaries. It is as if he has brought his sense of a mute (or absent) father into the consulting room and therefore cannot hear the counsellor's words.

Oral experience

Even during the earliest days of life the baby has already had considerable experience of boundary and containment.

Issues to do with feeding now become central, because this is where interaction so repeatedly and intensely takes place during this period. The mouth itself is a container, and thus can contain something else (the nipple, the thumb, or the corner of a blanket, for example) or can represent a lack of containment (vomiting, or an inability to latch on to the breast effectively). These are physical experiences, but they also seem to have the capacity to become a template for a whole range of feelings throughout childhood and on into adult life.

By the time a client comes into the consulting room, it will be hard for the practitioner to know what he brings of these early years. These might only emerge only over time, if then. Although in some instances it might not be appropriate to suggest links with the past (because of the short term nature of the work, what you judge the client can handle, or the depth at which the work takes place), nevertheless, it would be surprising if these links were not there in some form. For example, they might be seen in the vehemence with which your words are spat out or in the restless discomfort at being in a confined space with you.

Clinical example

Let us look in more detail at the first example – the client spitting out the counsellor's words so vehemently. The counsellor might respond by reintroducing what has been said in a more palatable form; notice the word 'palatable' and its association with the mouth and food. Perhaps the remark is still unacceptable, and is rejected again. Maybe the counsellor tries again, doing metaphorically what the mother might have done in introducing unfamiliar food – cutting it up into smaller chunks, mashing up the lumpy bits, or maybe even changing to a different brand name (a bit like using a different theoretical construct or explanation). Only later, when none of these alterations seems to have worked, does the counsellor 'catch on'. It turns out that it was not the content or consistency of the remark at all that was being rejected, but the emotional climate of the interaction that was disturbing and was being re-enacted in the consulting room. In other words, the patient experienced the counsellor's concern as anxiety and an attempt at control. From his vantage point, the original mother's determination to feed her baby so that he would grow vigorously was being inadvertently repeated in the counsellor's determination to find a way of helping her client to grow emotionally. The client 'spat out' her attempts much as he spat out his mother's early feeds, which he experienced as full of anxiety and control. He could not tell the counsellor what was wrong any more than he could as a baby verbalize his problem for his mother. The 'spitting out' was the only communication he had. He needed the counsellor, and previously his mother, to figure out what it meant.

Pre-oedipal

We use the term pre-oedipal to define the baby's earliest awareness of 'otherness', often occurring before there can be a conscious sense of separate persons or of triangular relationships. The vagueness of the term 'the other' is important, for it illustrates the fact that anything other than 'what is already' can become 'the other' for the baby. In its most concrete form this might be an 'other' person, but equally it could be a less familiar aspect of mother herself – the appearance of her walking away to an 'other' place, seen from an 'other' angle. Here, mother herself becomes 'the other.' It could also be the presence of a different emotional climate or an aspect of mother turned away, lost in her own thoughts. But the importance for us in the context of boundaries and containment is that 'other', by its very nature of 'otherness', brings the individual up against a boundary of what 'already is' or 'has been' and introduces the notion of difference and therefore the concept of 'twoness' or 'threeness' in its most primitive form. Again, this experience of 'other', happening so early in life, seems to form a template that affects later responses to experiences, and especially so during later years when Oedipal phantasies and triangular relationships take centre stage.

The emergence of teeth and the depressive position

Sometime in the first year, the baby will develop teeth. In the context of boundaries and containment, teeth can define a space or create a boundary in a manner different from gums or lips. The emergence of these new, harder, more sharply defined objects in the baby's mouth probably creates a greater consciousness of biting down, gripping, and holding on. These are all actions that result in the space within the mouth being separated from the space without. Kleinians speak of the emergence of the depressive position at this time. The baby begins to have the capacity to know that the mother who walks away and might frustrate his needs is the same mother who at other times can be nurturing and available for him. Metaphorically, he is allowing the 'good breast' (or the mother

19

who is there for him) and the 'bad breast' (the mother who is not) to belong to one person.

Clinical examples

In terms of the consulting room experience, the client might 'bite down on' our words or our presence. He might find it hard to leave at the end of the time and therefore make it hard for us to release that grip. He might hold on to our words tenaciously and perhaps anxiously, and be unable to grasp their meaning in the way that had been intended. He might be worried that if he 'lets go' or relaxes enough to 'take them in' (metaphorically 'swallowing the therapeutic food') it will somehow be lost. This might not be because of his counsellor's actual communications, but because he comes with the expectation based on early experience that what he does not hold firmly in place could disappear. So he brings to issues of boundary and containment, for example, a holiday break or a period of silence in the session, a response informed by this expectation of uncertainty. Of course, over time we hope that he will be affected by a different experience – our reliability; the fact that things talked about in one session are not necessarily lost and do turn up again even without his 'holding on'. He might find that he spontaneously remembers or that the counsellor sometimes remembers for him. Over time, he begins to have a reparative experience. He can relax in our presence and so can take in and be sustained by our 'food' in the therapeutic encounter.

Anal–urethral experience

The next 'peak' of development as far as issues of boundary and containment are concerned is the period of time (roughly eighteen months to three years) 'around' toilet training. Toilet training is only the outer, most visible sign of a complex period of separating out from the parents, of defining more precisely the boundary between the child's perception of himself and those in his world who are important but are not himself. It is almost as if the experience of the urine and faeces being at first inside and a part of his body and then outside and clearly separate from his body becomes a metaphor for so many of the experiences of this age – separating out, defining the boundary between me and mine, and you and yours, or not mine.

It is interesting that the toddler of this age shows great interest in opening and closing doors, opening and closing lids (particularly the toilet), or struggling with the garden gate long before he can reach the latch. These are all objects that define space by creating a boundary around it. This external differentiation and his interest in the process is a reflection of the inner process of differentiation that is going on at the same time.

Clinical example

Sometimes a parent does not recognize the underlying emotional struggle that accompanies the child's physical development. Likewise, the therapist can miss a client's unresolved struggles with separation that he might bring from this period of time. The therapist can get caught up in the therapeutic equivalent of putting things into the right container and lose sight of the fact that the patient might have been struggling to have an independent view from her and the maturation this can represent. Here it is all too easy to make badly timed interventions, hoping he will be a good, well-trained patient and not recognize the hurt that might inadvertently be inflicted on his emerging independence.

Oedipal experience

The oedipal stage of development is one of the more frequently talked about periods of life, both clinically among professionals and in the wider world among writers, film-makers, and the culture at large. Many parents will know the complications of three children playing; sooner rather than later (usually just when you have sat down with a cup of coffee!) you are called upon to mediate. Many of us remember ourselves or a child saying, 'But I want to marry Daddy (or Mummy) when I grow up!' Lovers know the pain of the third person who comes between them, creating an impossible triangular relationship.

Many of the broken relationships of the adult years stem from an unsatisfactory resolution of oedipal conflicts at the age of three or four. The child who has not found a way of holding on to one important relationship while maintaining another to someone equally important (perhaps his other parent) remains vulnerable later on. Just as the myth from which this developmental period takes its name suggests, the child caught in an oedipal entanglement with one parent might well 'kill off' the chance of fruitful encounter with the other. He cannot sustain both relationships and, therefore, a threesome just cannot exist. As a result, he cannot allow himself to experience his parents as a couple. As the classical story portrays so vividly, there are the seeds here of a terrible tragedy, because in the end one or both of the possible encounters must be killed off and with it the capacity for a depth of relationship with more than one love object at a time. It is not difficult to imagine how the complications of this period might affect boundary and containment issues.

Clinical example

Not infrequently, someone comes to counselling with the intention of exploring his inner thoughts and feelings only to find that there is a wall of guilt blocking access to the very area he had thought he was free to explore. This can happen because he finds himself about to confide to someone else intimate details about a relationship with a significant other. It is as if the counsellor is seen as a potentially significant person (the third side of an oedipal triangle) about to break in on a boundary that until now has contained only the client and his parent, partner, child, etc. In his thoughts there might have been a kind of unspoken, exclusive loyalty to this other that feels threatened by exposure, even in confidential surroundings, to a third person, the counsellor. Sometimes exploring the anxiety about the confidential nature of the setting is enough to free such ambivalence. However, if the conflict is deep-seated, it is much more likely that this particular 'no-go' area will have to remain in abeyance until a greater sense of trust has developed in the relationship. Sometimes, the relationship with a therapist who becomes emotionally important to the patient is felt as too great a threat to existing relationships and the work breaks down. In other cases, and especially where there is the opportunity for longer-term work, the client might

need to discover repeatedly and over time that the counsellor has no intention of breaking him and his partner
apart or of criticizing him for angry thoughts about his
partner.

Adolescence

Adolescence is a period of time when boundary and
containment issues can emerge at full intensity – at times,
like a Force Nine gale! There is something about the
passion of this period that feels like a continuation of the
passions of the two-year-old, having been put on hold or
in abeyance over the intervening years. In actuality, it is
more likely that the work of separating out has been going
on unnoticed in the background and now re-emerges on
centre stage. Anyone who has lived in close quarters with
an adolescent will know the degree to which the major
issues of this time are invariably about boundaries: boundaries of time – how late will they be out?; boundaries of
place – which pub or club is considered appropriate or not
by the parent?; boundaries of ownership – whose car is it
and who has the right to use it?; boundaries about whose
place it is anyway to make a judgement about any of these
questions. Teenagers tend to take action. If there is space
for the parents' point of view at all, it might be for about
thirty seconds with the television on while he is on the
phone to a friend already making arrangements about the
issue they wished to discuss before he phoned!

Clinical example

One can imagine various re-enactments of this period in
the consulting room. For instance, the therapist will have

24

made clear her dates for the Christmas break only to find that a particular client has not heard what she has tried to communicate and arrives during her holiday week. It might be that this person never moved beyond an adolescent non-communicating phase with a parent; he switched off and got a kind of secret space that way, under his control. Although he is not aware of the 'mistake', and is quite certain that it was the therapist's, he might, in coming during her free time, be indulging a wish to have a secret space with her. At the time this cannot be put into words, because he is caught up in an adolescent world where it would be unacceptable to let on to himself or to her that the contact matters that much. In any case, he could feel there is an issue of principle here. Who has the right over the counselling space? Just as the adolescent struggles with his parents over the car or the telephone, is the space the therapist's or his? At some level he might be saying that the session belongs exclusively to him and it is for him to decide when it happens, irrespective of her breaks or wishes. If he allows himself to 'hear' the holiday dates correctly, he will have to give up his control of the situation and face his feelings about the break 'breaking through' into his conscious thought.

Summary

This has been a brief look at some developmental issues and their implications for what might be brought to the consulting room years later. The illustrations are examples only. They could just as well have happened differently or have been linked to a different period of life; in fact, most probably not to just one experience, but to a whole complex mixture of experiences. They have been highlighted separately in this manner only to make it easier to demonstrate the possible dynamics.

How we respond to any of these situations will depend on the context of the work. With shorter-term or less intensive work, having a sense of the developmental issues that inform the individual's response in the here and now will, in the main, form a part of our understanding. It is held in the back of our minds, and in this indirect manner forms part of the framework in which we work. There might be no direct discussion of links between the here and now and the past, but it will still contribute to the boundary that we are providing around the work. Maybe this understanding functions like the presence of the unknown father referred to earlier. He is not there physically for the child but has an effect on the child's space because of being held in mind by the mother. In such work, our understanding of the dynamics affects the emotional climate of the session despite the fact that it is not spoken of directly.

There are some people in longer-term counselling, and many in psychotherapy, for whom the links between the past and the present are a helpful means of making sense of disturbing feelings and behaviour. What we say and how we say it is beyond the scope of this book, but it will be determined in part by the nature of the boundaries around the work. These will include the experience of the practitioner, the nature of the supervision, the frequency at which the patient is being seen, whether it is in the beginning, middle, or end of the session, whether it is in a session before a weekend break or followed closely by another session. It will also depend on the emotional climate of that particular day for both the counsellor and the client.

CHAPTER THREE

NUTS AND BOLTS

'How can I tell you anything. I don't know you; this isn't a real relationship.'

Most therapists will hear some version of these words in the course of their daily work. To an extent the patient is correct – the relationship between therapist and patient does not feel like a customary social encounter because it is not one. It is a therapeutic encounter to which both parties pay a particular kind of attention. The therapist attempts to maintain a therapeutic attitude in which to listen and talk to the client in as non-judgemental a way as possible. In this chapter we look at how the therapist's careful attention to concrete boundaries helps to construct and maintain the container within which both therapist and patient can feel safe to work. These boundaries are shaped in the main by contractual agreements such as time, money, and space, and it is aspects of these that are considered here.

Assessment

The patient has negotiated his way through cultural and personal ambivalence, obtained a referral to a qualified counsellor or psychotherapist, and the first assessment appointment has been made.

The assessment is likely to include:

- the presenting problem, i.e., the reason the patient is seeking treatment;
- an outline of the patient's personal and family history which led to his seeking psychotherapy;
- whether or not the patient has a supportive enough network of family, colleagues, or friends;
- whether the patient would benefit from the type of therapy being offered and, if not, which kind of therapeutic approach would be more appropriate (e.g., open-ended or short-term, psychodynamic or cognitive).

It is probable that the focus of work established at the beginning of therapy will have changed shape by the end. This might be for a whole host of conscious and unconscious reasons, which we shall discuss in Chapter Eight. It could also be because the client has 'outgrown' what the present counsellor can do for him or because he needs something different from what is being offered. Within the mental health field there are different approaches and specialities that might be more or less appropriate for different clients.

Sometimes a judgement can be made about this at the beginning of the work and a referral made at that point. In other instances, the most appropriate kind of help will only emerge in the process of the work, as if the work itself were a kind of ongoing assessment. In some cases, the practitioner will wear more than one hat. He might have worked with the client in a counselling capacity before having also trained as a psychotherapist. He might decide that the client who originally came with a particular problem in mind is now open to working in greater depth. Given his advanced training, he considers continuing to work with him. On the other hand, there might be constraints placed on the practioner by funding, by institutional guidelines, or by a training that did not include more intensive work. All these factors can make 'referral out' necessary.

In the case of referral, there will be an end to the therapist's involvement with the client. The work will continue elsewhere. How and whether that work proceeds will depend to some extent on how the referral process is handled. The therapist now becomes an intermediary, responsible for both an ending and for a link to a new beginning elsewhere. Depending on the setting and the amount of control over it, there might be only one session to facilitate the transfer, a number of sessions, or, in the ideal case, whatever amount of time the therapist and client feel is necessary. Obviously, the time available will determine how the ending unfolds. Another determining factor will be the capacity of the client to consider what is happening and to acknowledge it at this particular stage in the therapeutic process.

The duration of the present therapy is also likely to affect the intensity of the client's feelings in coming to an end. However, it is important to recognize that attachment can also take place within a very short period of time, sometimes instantaneously. It can happen without even meeting in person. A therapist's name might have been suggested to a potential client. He might have had only telephone contact and have been told the therapist does not have a vacancy. The therapist who is subsequently seen can be felt to be second best, never coming up to the expectations bestowed on the first therapist in his absence. Equally, someone comes for one session and then feels terribly displaced by the suggestion that it might be more appropriate for him to go elsewhere. Because of the nature of his need, he may have formed an instant bond. Even with very short or minimal contact, there is the task of helping the client to come to an end and to invest enough elsewhere for the referral to work.

At times, and despite our best efforts, the link cannot be made and the referral fails. The patient might refuse to move, consciously or unconsciously angry at what is perceived as a rejection. What the therapist attempts to set up for him is then rejected in retaliation, or the client, having told his story, might be unable or unwilling to tell it all over again to someone else. A referral might repeat too exactly an earlier experience of betrayal that he might or might not be able to disclose, or even recognize, at this stage. In such instances, the therapist might have to decide whether, despite not being ideal, there is good enough fit with the client's needs to proceed with the work himself (especially if there is sound supervision in place), or whether he needs to allow the client to stop prematurely, hoping that he might start again in the future.

In some instances, patients in therapy within the setting of an institution continue to be seen by a succession of practitioners rather than being referred outside for the long-term uninterrupted work they so clearly need. Clinically, we must question this practice and wonder whether this is an indication of institutional 'omnipotence'. When a patient's need is compromised in this manner, we must ask whether the system is unable to face its own lack of resources or, perhaps, its envy of other practitioners. Just as our clients sometimes have to face their omnipotence, so therapists and institutions must not assume they can do everything. We would go so far as to say that it is unethical not to let a client go if it appears that he would benefit from a different kind of help available elsewhere. The therapist or institution that has a clear view of what it can and cannot do makes an important conceptual boundary around the work.

In this regard, it may be that therapeutic work has been affected by the inclusive nature of our present culture. Inclusion has had many positive outcomes, but it has also led to the assumption that everyone can do everything and to a lack of differentiation. We are all familiar with the growth of supermarkets and how their selling of everything under one roof has contributed to the demise of the specialist High Street shop. On a smaller scale, each shop now wants to sell a range of goods to corner the market. The bank sells insurance. The newsagent sells flowers. The hairdresser sells greetings cards. The list is endless. Perhaps it is not surprising that the mental health professional is also tempted to make claims for his 'shop' to suit every passer-by.

Assessment is a more complicated process than we can do justice to in this context. The curriculum of a recognized training and the relevant counselling/psychotherapy literature will provide more comprehensive treatment of the subject.

The first session

If an assessment of the patient's suitability for therapeutic work has not already been made, the first meeting(s) usually become an assessment. Once the assessment has taken place and mutually convenient times and fees have been agreed, these early sessions will include a discussion of therapeutic expectations. However, there will also need to be a discussion about practical arrangements. This will include the length of individual sessions (usually fifty minutes, but this can vary), whether a fee will be charged for sessions cancelled by the patient when the therapist is working, the timing and arrangements for payment of accounts, and the name and address of the patient's GP to inform him that the patient has started counselling or psychotherapy. Where appropriate, it should also include information about travel, parking, and whether a waiting-room is available. Some therapists provide written guide-lines to supplement what is said to the patient.

The patient might ask the therapist where she trained and how long she has been in practice. The patient is enti-tled to this information, even if the therapist might also want to explore why the patient wants to know.

Beginnings and ends of sessions

Patients can feel uncomfortable on entering the consult-ing room and having to negotiate the space with the ther-apist. This can be a reflection of many personal anxieties and difficulties, but it also reflects the common experience that entry, especially in the early stages of therapy, *is* diffi-cult. For many people the beginning is daunting – they are unsure whether they are welcome or not, or afraid of what they might reveal of themselves in an unguarded moment. They can be paralysed by other fears, such as boring the therapist, or perhaps wishing they had never ventured into this experience in the first place.

Case example

A patient could not make his usual session time the following week and the therapist agreed to see him on another evening when he did not usually work. However, the therapist forgot to make a note of this in his diary and subsequently arranged for a friend to come on the same evening as the patient. When the doorbell rang, the therapist opened the door. In the dimly-lighted hallway, the therapist could see only an outline, not the features of the person at the door. The therapist's mind had composed the image of the friend and warmly greeted him. When a different person came into view the therapist suddenly realized that reality did not correspond with the expected image; he had momentarily failed to recognize his patient.

This is an example of what we see being influenced by what we expect to see. Therefore Bion advises us:

> The first point is for the analyst to impose on himself a positive discipline of eschewing memory and desire. I do not mean that 'forgetting' is enough: what is required is a positive act of refraining from memory and desire. [Bion, 1988, p. 31]

Bion challenges the therapist to refrain from thinking he knows the patient on the basis of past meetings so that he remains open to finding out about the patient in the present meeting. The complementary 'rule' for the patient is that he tries to talk about whatever is on his mind at that moment.

Similarly, patients can find the ending and leaving of the session difficult. They might try to overcome the difficulty by enquiring after the therapist, 'Are you doing anything nice this weekend,' or by suddenly revealing "I've never told anyone this before but . . .' right on the dot of time. Undeniably, the process of coming and going is hard, but it is important that the therapist recognizes this and does not try to change the phenomenon by attempting to 'make it better'. Trainees initially wonder whether they should end a session on time if their patient is still distressed. Comments such as 'we can talk about that next time' are sometimes felt to be necessary and may help to contain the immediate anxiety. However, they can also create an expectation that the patient should continue with this issue at the next session, even though it may no longer be of immediate concern.

Time

A crucial aspect of time in psychodynamic work is that it encompasses both conscious and unconscious time. Unconscious 'time' has the quality of timelessness. Freud, in describing the characteristics of the unconscious, writes,

> The processes of the system Ucs. are timeless, i.e. they are not ordered temporally, are not altered by the passage of time; they have no reference to time at all. Reference to time is bound up ... with the work of the system Cs. [Freud, 1915, p. 187]

One implication of this is that present, past, and future can all be experienced within the time span of a single session as if they all existed in the present. Thus, a patient's inner experience of time affects the meaning attributed to what is happening in the outer time of the session. It is fascinating to observe how. in the unconscious. different time intervals can be equated.

Case example

An extremely punctual patient arrived two minutes late for a session. Usually she was exactly on time. In discussion it emerged that the two minutes represented a two-week break in the therapy which she had been anticipating. In the unconscious, as in dreams, time is experienced in a different way to consciousness. In this case two minutes and two weeks were equated. It was as if she were saying, 'If you lose two weeks of our time, I will retaliate and lose two minutes of the session.'

Apart from the actual words expressed, how the patient uses the beginning and end of the session can be instructive. Some arrive late, some early. Some look at a watch continually, others not at all. Fifty minutes might be experienced as too long, too short, or just right. The same patient can experience each of these reactions on different occasions. If a patient communicates in this non-verbal way, it is important to try to understand what is being experienced. For instance, a patient who continually arrived early was, unconsciously, seeking to intrude on imagined siblings.

Another who arrived late was, unconsciously, re-enacting a pattern of deprivation. In a session when a patient said very little the therapist assumed he was withholding something. In reality, the patient had been conducting an intense, silent conversation and felt the session much too short. A patient who experienced a session as extra long imagined that the therapist was treating him as a special case and allowing extra time.

Patients react differently to the end of the session. One patient experienced this as a rejection, phantasizing that the therapist was all too relieved to be rid of her. It emerged that in her phantasy the patient was relating to a mother whom she experienced as never having enough time for her. Another patient, believing himself subject to the therapist's power and control, felt relieved to get out of his sessions. Patients' attempts to extend the time might be a non-verbal indication that they can only get what they need by stealing it. Patients who repeatedly do this might be indicating that they want to address something they have so far neglected, or perhaps that they need more sessions per week. In the latter case, the counsellor might begin to think about referring the patient to a psycho-therapist or analyst who is trained in more intensive work. In any event, what is important is that the therapist tries to understand what is being done to the boundary and talks about this in a meaningful way with the patient.

Usually the time of the session, once agreed, is kept as fixed as possible. However, many patients today have to work shifts, or are not in a position to refuse extra demands at the end of the working day. Within reason, it is sometimes necessary to be flexible. Nevertheless, Tuesday afternoon is not the same as Friday morning, and it is important to keep in mind that feelings of loss can occur with even a seemingly minor change. This can be the case even if the patient is relieved that the request for change has been accommodated. It can be tempting for both therapist and patient to avoid feelings to do with such change and to assume that everything is the same as long as eqivalent time has been provided. The novelty of coming at a different time can also be stimulating, titil-lating, or anxiety provoking, among other reactions. Sometimes a patient who usually comes after work and finds it difficult to avoid focusing on work issues can access more personal material in a session rearranged to an early morning time.

Jung's concept of synchronicity is an interesting contri-bution to our understanding of time. He conceptualizes synchronicity as a symbolic connection between apparently unconnected events, or meaningful coincidence. That is, two events may coincide, but one has not caused the other. He writes,

> Synchronistic events rest on the simultaneous occurrence of two different psychic states. One of them is the normal, probable state (i.e. the one that is causally explicable) and the other, the critical experience, is the one that cannot be derived causally from the first. [Jung, 1952, par. 444]

In the same paper Jung says, 'Synchronicity therefore means the simultaneous occurrence of a certain psychic state with one or more external events which appear as meaningful parallels to the momentary subjective state . . .' (Jung, 1952, par. 441).

Clinical example

A young man was referred for psychotherapy to determine whether this would be a suitable form of treatment for his depression. The consultation went badly. Although the young man rephrased everything the therapist said, and appeared very annoyed with the whole procedure, he denied ever feeling angry about anything. The therapist struggled with his own growing feelings of irritation and anger. After reflection on the unsatisfactory nature of the first consultation, another was offered. The young man agreed, but on the way to the second consultation was involved in a car accident and ended up going to a casualty department at the session time. The next appointment was cancelled because one of his children fell down a slide. Again the man found himself in the casualty department at the corresponding time.

After consultation with colleagues, the therapist recognized that for this young man even a consultation about entering a therapeutic relationship was felt unconsciously to be too dangerous. Thinking about the meaning of these simultaneous events led to an understanding that there was a meaning in the timing of the accidents that related to the unconscious fears of this young man, despite the fact that the accidents were not directly caused by his anxiety.

Money

Money can be a complex area of therapeutic work. The level of the fee can be a barrier to some patients. Most training organizations make provision for this by providing reduced fee schemes. Some (usually time-limited) psychotherapy and counselling is available within the National Health Service (NHS). There is considerable cost attached to NHS therapy, in the form of salaries and overheads, even though this is not reflected directly in fees charged to the patient.

Fees charged in private practice define the formal nature of the transaction by making it clear that the therapist is providing a professional service: what is purchased is time, space, and the therapist's skilled and committed involvement with the patient. The time and space are not usually transferable if a patient is ill, or misses a session. It is common practice that sessions which are not attended still have to be paid for – because they remain available to the patient.

Patients in therapy, as stated previously, enter unconscious time. Because of this there can be a reawakening of infantile defences and attitudes. Therefore, money can assume an importance and acquire a meaning that has very little to do with actual resources. Careful consideration of the patient's attitude to money can reveal a great deal about his inner world.

Clinical example

A professional woman expressed her very great desire to begin therapy but an equal conviction that she could not afford it. This puzzled the therapist, as the woman had no dependants, reasonably secure employment, and no immediate debts. The therapist was concerned, as the patient was clearly suffering a great deal of emotional pain. She decided to investigate the financial situation in some detail. The patient explained to the therapist how she arranged her finances: she paid all bills with standing orders and direct debits, and money was put aside for holidays, clothes, etc. On the face of it this sounded very organized and reasonable, but the result was that in dividing the money so carefully the patient had no concept of the 'whole' of what she earned. When that was considered she realized that the money for therapy could be released by slightly reducing the amount being saved. The way the patient treated her income could be seen as a description of her own inner experience – feeling broken up and without internal resourcefulness, 'broke'. She allowed no money for the therapy just as she allowed no money for her immediate needs. In dividing it up she was, paradoxically, re-enacting her inner sense of deprivation.

The symbolic significance that money has for each individual can be most illuminating. Another patient, who could quite easily afford to pay, withheld fees because of a strong feeling that the therapist was stealing from and exploiting him: the therapist was not the 'mother' he hoped for – the mother who has no needs of her own and gives unconditionally, without being paid. A patient, who also seemed to be in conflict over payment, found the money once her resentment towards the therapist was articulated.

Spending money on themselves can leave some patients feeling overly guilty. They might think of themselves as unworthy of such expenditure, or worry that they are having an experience other family members do not have. Such patients might also believe the therapist is entirely dependent on their money and therefore feel overly responsible for her welfare.

Money can also be problematic for the therapist. Therapists working in private practice need to eat, pay their own bills, have sufficient non-working time, and enjoy a reasonable standard of living. Yet it is sometimes difficult to admit this. The therapist is not immune to phantasies of self-sufficiency, of being 'able to manage', or undermined by the phantasy that it is the duty of someone in a 'caring profession' to sacrifice his own needs. He might believe that he is not good enough because his patients cannot afford the high fees that other therapists command. He might be unable to charge the standard fee because of such feelings of unworthiness, or shame at his own need for money. On the other hand, an unrealistic sense of entitlement, and of his own importance, might lead him to set fees that are prohibitively high for ordinary patients.

The setting of appropriate fees is therefore something that does need careful thought, and perhaps consultation with colleagues. Of course, there are also situations where the cost of therapy is covered by a salary, and money does not come into the session in so concrete a form. Nevertheless, the question of what value the session has for the patient, and of how much the therapist thinks it is worth, is still relevant.

The consulting room and its environs

The concrete reality of therapeutic space is that the consulting room is a room belonging to, rented by, or, in an institution, assigned to the therapist. Any room that is regularly used acquires a sense of belonging for the therapist for whom it is designated. Thus, the room and its furnishings can reveal much information about the therapist, as well as providing material for the client's phantasy.

Therapists need to be aware of the effect of the room's location in the outside world. The patients of therapists working in a psychiatric hospital might be troubled by the presence of more seriously ill patients in the waiting area. Some patients might have the phantasy that mental illness is as contagious as, for example, the common cold.

When a therapist is working from home, noises of family life can sometimes be overheard in the consulting room. Because these noises are associated with the therapist's family, they can arouse oedipal anxieties in the patient. Although it can be useful to learn about the patient's phantasies, occasionally too great an anxiety can lead to acting out or a breakdown of the therapy. For this reason, considerable thought needs to be given to how the room can become a safe container for the patient. It is important that the therapist's private living area be as separate as possible, so that the impact of family life is minimized. Access to a lavatory is important, and a waiting area, where possible.

Opinions vary about the arrangement of the room. Most therapists sit at a slight angle to the patient so he has a choice of whether or not to look at the therapist. If the therapist has been trained in more intensive work, there will also be a couch.

Some therapists think the furnishings should be invested with as little personal significance as possible. If an object is too important to the therapist the aim of interpretations can be to protect the object rather than to understand the client's projections.

Clinical example

A therapist introduced a small Victorian table to her consulting room, thinking that it would make the room more attractive. One day a patient, in a particularly angry phase of the therapy, threatened to break up the table. The therapist found her concern divided between preserving the table and understanding the patient's aggressive feelings. It was, therefore, impossible to maintain an 'analytic attitude' and to interpret, non-judgementally, the passionate anger the patient felt towards the therapist.

Therapists need to be aware of their own need for a safe area to work. In this case, the threat of violence quickly receded once the therapist became conscious of her split loyalties, and was able to interpret this. But if a patient persists in the type of abuse and/or threatening behaviour that makes it impossible to work or that unduly frightens the therapist (even if such situations are very rare), it might be necessary to find a way to bring the therapy to an end.

The therapist's need for safe containment can be neglected, especially in 'caring' organizations such as hospitals. Here, the needs of the patient are usually considered paramount, and the fact that all treatment takes place within relationships might not be taken into account. Attention to the boundaries of the container and to the needs of the therapist make the work safer for both therapist and patient. This is supported by a professional training and ongoing supervision, but it is also necessary for therapists to have undergone personal counselling or therapy in order to have reached sufficient understanding of their own personal boundaries.

There is also physical space outside the consulting room where the therapist might meet his patient. Usually therapist and patient do not meet intentionally outside the therapeutic 'hour', but a patient who lives in the same area might be met in local shops or other facilities. Professional patients are sometimes encountered at conferences or talks. The therapeutic relationship is present between therapist and patient whether or not they are in the consulting room. When meetings do occur, some way of politely acknowledging each other might need to be negotiated. Whatever happens, it is important to talk about such meetings within the context of a subsequent session.

Clinical example

A young male patient went to open the door of the consulting room at the end of a session. The doorknob came off in his hand, leaving him and the therapist trapped in the room. The room opened on to a balcony adjoining a neighbour's balcony. Both were able to climb over on to next door's balcony and were allowed through by a bemused neighbour.

The importance of this event lies not only in that it happened, but in the subsequent thinking that could be done about it. The material (the actual event) could be thought about by both therapist and patient to explore its psychological meaning. This was possible because the 'container', though broken at this point, had been safe enough for the work to proceed when the unexpected occurred.

When something so unusual happens many resonances are found within the patient's past and the internal state of the therapist. This young man had spent many hope-less hours in his childhood trapped with his disturbed father. He insisted on locking the doors, drawing the curtains, and not letting the boy out to face the suspected dangers of the outside world. In this event both patient and therapist had 'relived' the trauma, but, in this case, a way out was found. With time, the patient was able to understand and to come to terms with his fears of being trapped if he committed himself to any form of relation-ship. Unconsciously, he had feared that other people, like his father, would restrict his freedom and want to 'keep him at home'.

Jung emphasized the importance of the therapist's awareness of his own involvement in the therapeutic process. He saw both patient and therapist as being in the 'vas bene clausum' (well-sealed vessel) of the relation-ship. In the above case, the therapist also had to face her part in the event. She had not paid attention to signif-icant details – such as the gradually loosening doorknob – that might have alerted her. With this patient she had been concentrating on the positive aspects of the work, such as his regular attendance and his willingness to understand her interpretations. With another patient she might have questioned such compliance, but here she had, unconsciously, sought to avoid being seen as a parent 'with a screw loose' who might try to trap him. This unconscious denial prevented her from recognizing that she was in danger of re-enacting the role of such a parent. This became real by her inadvertently locking the patient in with her.

We have been describing some aspects of the boundary that contains both therapist and patient. There are also boundaries *between* therapist and patient. Here, it is relevant to mention the convention in psychodynamic therapies that physical contact between therapist and patient does not occur. However, in some cultures it is common practice to shake hands or even to hug someone on arrival or departure. Explaining that this is against the therapist's Code of Ethics might make a refusal less personally hurtful, but it is also important to explore what the 'refusal' means to the patient. Of course, therapists working with children, or physically ill and/or dying patients, may modify their practice, but it remains important to understand why this is happening. These and other aspects of Professional boundaries are explored in Chapter Seven.

Telephone, e-mail and text contacts

Therapists sometimes have to cancel sessions at short notice. Patients might also need to convey factual information between sessions. But telephone conversations between sessions can be problematic. If the conversation strays into emotional areas it can be difficult to contain.

The patient might enter a free-associative state, but without the containment ordinarily provided by the session.

A different situation arises when the phone contact results from an emotional crisis. The therapist might need to provide an emergency boundary by indicating a time limit to his availability, and reminding the distressed and possibly confused patient about the existing structure of his sessions.

Occasionally, a patient might not be able to attend a session and request fifty minutes of telephone time instead. How this is dealt with varies between individual therapists but, again, it is important to consider the effect on the ongoing therapeutic relationship. In general, it is better to contain the conversation, reminding the patient of his next available session. If necessary, and if the therapist can do so, an earlier appointment might be offered. Telephone counselling is a skill in its own right. In any case, fifty minutes on the phone, where it can be difficult to maintain the usual silences of the consulting room, can be overly intense. A prolonged conversation might arouse, rather than contain, the patient's distress.

Modern technology might encourage some patients to want to use e-mails and text messaging with their therapist. It would be hard not to see this as an attempt to have a more personal relationship with the therapist and to wonder why a phone call is not sufficient. As with previous situations, it is important, when possible, to bring what is being expressed unconsciously into the consulting room.

Note-keeping

Note-keeping has become an important issue for therapists (see Chapter Six). As a minimum, notes should indicate the name and address of the patient and when he started and finished therapy. More extensive process notes, such as those used in supervision, need to be destroyed as soon as they are no longer needed. Some therapists also choose to record significant sessions, such as when the patient expresses suicidal ideation or when the therapist gives him holiday dates. Some therapists prefer to keep notes of the session separately from the official record. However, if notes exist they cannot be destroyed once a legal process has begun. It is essentially a matter of personal choice and practice, but the therapist does need to keep in mind that a court of law can subpoena notes and, in general, they have to be made available.

CHAPTER FOUR

THE CONTAINING MIND

Within the more tangible boundaries of therapeutic work, discussed in the previous chapter, reside the less tangible boundaries, the relationship between the therapeutic couple and the mental space available to therapist and patient being the most important.

The contents of the therapist's mind

The therapist's thought processes will have been influenced in part by the theoretical model or models he is using to think about his patient's material. Although Jung tried not to promote particular techniques for therapy, he did acknowledge the need for the therapist to be both knowledgeable as well as flexible in responding to the patient. Knowledge of theory, received through a recognized professional training, helps to prevent the therapist basing interventions on personal opinion. However, as Jung advocated, theoretical ideas should emerge from an understanding of the patient's material and not from an imposition of the therapist's thinking (Jung, 1935, par. 8).

Methodology and theoretical stance operate 'behind the scenes', framing his responses to the patient's material. They are 'behind the scenes' because they are not known about directly by the patient. Yet, they provide a frame of reference for all the reading, lectures, theoretical discussions, previous work, and papers that have contributed to the therapist's training over time. From this reservoir of experience and learning, the therapist extracts meaning to fit what the patient brings. This boundary is somewhat porous. For example, as the patient begins talking about the significance of his childhood pet, the therapist might find himself remembering the dog he also owned as a child. Of course, the therapist does not say, 'That sounds like the dog I had as a boy. I loved him dearly.' On the other hand, he might use the experience indirectly to recollect how meaningful a child's pet can be.

The methodology, largely acquired through training and subsequent supervision, provides a means of orientation to the patient's material. For example, most psychodynamic practitioners will have learned (sometimes with difficulty) to wait and 'not know' in response to their patient's communications. This particular method provides an important space for the patient to elaborate his feelings and for the therapist to consider what has been said before responding. It is an important boundary, providing time and openness for the therapeutic encounter. It is, of course, important that it does not function too rigidly.

The timing of interpretations – that is, when to respond to the patient's material – can be difficult to get 'right'. A patient might begin to explore an area when the therapist, unable to contain his own understanding, rushes in. This can be a kind of showing off and/or an inability to wait for the patient to reach his own conclusions. The patient can feel his inner space has been invaded. He has not been allowed to discover his own ability to know himself.

For example, a therapist hearing that a patient has suffered sexual abuse might assume that this issue would be the focus of the therapy. But for the patient, talking can mean reliving the shame and denigration of the original experience. It can mean re-experiencing the voyeuristic sadism of the abuser in the therapist. The therapist's relative silence might give the patient the impression that his ambivalent response to the therapist has disappointed him. The patient's reluctance might be interpreted as 'he will not talk', or 'he cannot make use of the opportunity to help himself'. In such circumstances, the patient can end up feeling more abused. He may have come to therapy not to deal with the abuse issue directly but to re-discover a safe place in which to explore his feelings.

The therapist's mental space, largely inaccessible to the patient, is most in evidence when the therapist makes an interpretation. In talking about a patient's material, the therapist reveals that he has been having thoughts or making links that the patient has not previously known. This capacity to make use of the mind has been understood and described in various ways by different theoreticians.

Triangular space

Freud's Oedipus Complex provides a means of understanding the dynamics of 'threesomes'. The triangle of mother, father, and child, and their inevitable conflicts, involves the developing child in experiences of excitement, envy, jealousy, rage, or fear in relation to his observation and/or phantasy of his parents' sexual relationship, a relationship which excludes the child. Britton, a contemporary Freudian, writes:

> The acknowledgement by the child of the parents' relationship with each other unites his psychic world, limiting

it to one shared with his two parents in which different object relationships can exist. The closure of the Oedipal triangle by the recognition of the link joining the parents provides a limiting boundary for the internal world. It creates what I call a 'triangular space' – i.e., a space bounded by the three persons of the oedipal situation and all their potential relationships. It includes, therefore, the possibility of being a participant in a relationship and observed by a third person as well as being an observer of a relationship between two people. [Britton, 1989, p. 86]

Triangular space can also be thought of as an individual's relationship to two varying states of mind. Britton describes how the infant's capacity to manage the Oedipal triangle is important in the development of thought and the toleration of frustration. In the consulting room the existence of triangular space might mean the patient being able to tolerate the therapist having a partner or, perhaps, a mind capable of thoughts that exclude the patient.

The Transcendent Function is a rather complex Jungian concept that describes the capacity of the mind to bridge conscious and unconscious thought. This bridging aspect functions as a 'third hand' for the therapist. Describing the Transcendent Function as a 'third hand' applies the Oedipal concept of the 'threeness', not in its usual sense as applying to three different persons or entities, but to three aspects of one thing: the therapist's mind (the conscious, the unconscious, and the bridge between or the Transcendent Function). The therapist makes use of the Transcendent Function (or perhaps it is more accurate to say the Transcendent Function makes use of the therapist, because the bridging process takes place spontaneously in response to the patient's material). An image or thought forms in the therapist's mind that has the potential for insight into previously inaccessible material. The therapist, finding her conscious mind insufficient to understand the patient, is aided by the spontaneous intervention of the Transcendent Function to help make sense of it. The therapist cannot will this to happen; rather she is the recipient of its activity through a general sense of openness to the experiences (Jung, 1958).

Container–contained

In his description of the container and the contained, the psychoanalyst Wilfred Bion provides a model of how mother and child, therapist and patient use each other's minds (Bion, 1970, p. 72ff). The infant projects into the mother overwhelming feelings that he needs understood. It is essential to the infant that the mother does some work on these feelings (consciously or unconsciously tries to understand their meaning) before returning them in a form he can incorporate. In order to do this, the mother/ therapist must have an area of internal triangular space (the thinking container) within which to transform the received material before giving back (interpreting) feelings in a more digestible form. Similarly, Winnicott writes of the infant's experience of time being managed by the holding and containing function of the mother (Winnicott, 1985, pp. 76–77). Didier Anzieu describes how the child comes to experience his skin as an interface boundary between internal and external. This provides an experience of '. . . an encompassing volume in which he feels himself bathed, the surface and the volume affording him the experience of a container' (Anzieu, 1989, p. 37).

Jung's approach emphasizes the relationship between therapist and client as the container within which both are working. He uses an analogy to marriage to help explain these dynamics. In the marital relationship the partners project different aspects of themselves into each other. As a healthy relationship develops, both partners begin to withdraw these projections and become more able to experience the other as someone different and not an extension of themselves (Jung, 1931b, par. 331–342). In a similar manner, therapeutic work involves the patient unconsciously projecting aspects of himself into the therapist, his therapeutic partner. In other words, he makes assumptions about the therapist that are actually about himself. Gradually, the therapist understands the nature of these projections. One of the objects of psychotherapy and some kinds of counselling is to think and talk about these projections with the patient so the projected qualities can eventually be 'returned'. The extent and depth to which this can be done depends on the nature and intensity of the therapy and the ability of the patient to 'hear' such communications.

Fordham reminds us that the patient is not contained within the mind of the therapist as a passive object awaiting treatment, nor is the outcome of the treatment the sole responsibility of the therapist. The patient also plays a vital part. He writes,

> . . . it is sometimes maintained that a patient is healed by the analyst's love, and that in being a 'good parent', he can redress the faults of his patient's upbringing or heal the patient's self image. It is an idea of the infant self-representation that has become damaged by his mother's treatment of him. That, though it can happen, implies far

too innocent an understanding of mother–infant interaction; it leaves out the infant's part in creating a good enough mother. The study of mothers and infants demonstrates clearly that a mother can be a good enough mother with one child and not with another in the same family, or that an infant can virtually create a good enough mother by the precision of his signs and the apparent knowledge of what his mother can tolerate and what she cannot. [Fordham, 1985, p. 216]

Transference and countertransference

An understanding of the power of the transference led early psychoanalysts to begin to establish guidelines (boundaries) for the treatment of their patients. Freud warns against enacting the role projected on to the therapist by the patient and advises the latter to stick to the path of interpretation rather than action. He writes,

> However much the analyst might be tempted to become a teacher, model and ideal for other people and to create men in his own image, he should not forget that that is not his task in the analytic relationship, and indeed that he will be disloyal to his task if he allows himself to be led on by his inclinations. If he does, he will only be repeating a mistake of the parents who crushed their child's independence by their influence and he will only be replacing the patient's earlier dependence by a new one. In all his attempts at improving and educating the patient the analyst should respect his individuality. [Freud, 1940a, p. 175]

Jung understood the great importance of the patient's effect on the therapist (i.e., the countertransference), both as a therapeutic tool and as a potential to disturb, even injure, the therapist. He writes:

> In any effective psychological treatment the doctor is bound to influence the patient; but this influence can only take place if the patient has a reciprocal influence on the doctor. You can exert no influence if you are not susceptible to influence. It is futile for the doctor to shield himself from the influence of the patient and to surround himself with a smoke-screen of fatherly and professional authority. By so doing he only denies himself the use of a highly important organ of information. The patient influences him unconsciously none the less, and brings about changes in the doctor's unconscious which are well known to many psychotherapists: psychic disturbances or even injuries peculiar to the profession, a striking illustration of the patient's almost 'chemical' action. One of the best known symptoms of this kind is the counter-transference evoked by the transference. [Jung, 1931a, par. 163]

This projection of feelings inevitably occurs as part of a therapeutic endeavour because it is the unconscious means by which the patient communicates with the therapist. The therapist's experience of such projections form the basis of his countertransference. The countertransference is initially an unconscious communication and, if it is not brought to consciousness and understood by the therapist, can result in acting out. In many breach of ethics' cases the therapist has become unconsciously identified with the patient's projections, thereby losing the separateness of his own mind. What should be symbolic becomes concrete. Talk about intimacy becomes confused with actual intimacy. What has been lost is triangular space, the sense of the 'third', represented by the therapist's mind (internal triangular apace) as well as his professional organization and its Code of Ethics (external triangular space). When there is no triangular space there is no containment for projections and acting out can occur.

CHAPTER FIVE

BOUNDARIES WITHIN
ORGANIZATIONAL SETTINGS

The internal, mental boundaries of the therapist's mind can become even more important within settings outside the somewhat protected environment of the private consulting room. This chapter gives a series of clinical examples (based on actual situations) that illustrate how ethical and boundary issues can dramatically affect, and be affected by, the workplace.

An NHS out-patient
psychotherapy service

As part of her continuing professional development, a community psychiatric nurse worked psychotherapeutically with a woman who had been sexually abused. Although they had met for some considerable time and their relationship seemed a good one, the patient did not show any significant improvement, particularly in her ability to relate to others. She remained convinced that people did not like her. She did not express any feeling, particularly anger.

In supervision it emerged that the CPN behaved much as she might in her nursing practice, where the understanding of boundaries was very different. Instead of waiting to see how the patient might wish to begin the session, she greeted her, asked how she was and how her week had been. At the end the CPN would touch her arm and wish her a good week. The supervisor suggested that the CPN apply stricter boundaries – not open the conversation, touch the patient, or wish her a pleasant week ahead.

Initially, the patient was very upset. She accused the CPN of not touching her any more because she was disgusted by her sexual abuse. She said the silence at the beginning was an ordeal. She wanted to leave therapy but her GP advised her to continue. After a while, the patient began to understand that despite this change the therapist was prepared to think about her feelings and her anger. She was not rejecting the patient, but providing a setting where these could be expressed. As the patient began to feel contained by the therapist's firmer boundaries, she felt safer in expressing her feelings. This enabled her to take more risks in her personal life. Gradually, her relationships improved to the extent that the therapy was able to end. From the beginning the therapeutic relationship was at risk of failing because of a lack of appropriate boundaries. Had it not been for skilled supervision and the GP's intervention the therapy might have continued forever with little or no improvement.

A hostel for young homeless people

Brian began working in a hostel for young homeless people. He appreciated the atmosphere in the project and the staff's awareness of the emotional needs of residents. They placed great importance on the construction and maintenance of boundaries because they were aware that residents had missed out on secure boundaries in childhood. The building's external boundaries were very prominent, because it backed on to a solid rock face while at the front was a busy main road. Brian was impressed that the internal boundaries seemed just as solid. The hostel was an old family hotel converted into bed-sits. There were many locked doors and each resident had a key to his own bedroom. Staff retained keys to other important areas – the kitchen, fridge, and food cupboard, etc.

There were also significant boundaries to do with time. Residents could stay for only six months. Appointments had to be made to see their key worker. There was a curfew at night. It was expected that rent would be paid on time. Chores had to be done promptly. These time boundaries were the most difficult for residents, and staff understood this as an indication that self-discipline had been minimal in their family homes and time therefore had little meaning.

Despite the apparent emphasis on boundaries, Brian soon realized that a lot of drugs were being smoked in the hostel. He found the staff's acceptance of this worrying, because the hostel rules explicitly stated that substance abuse was grounds for eviction. However, colleagues reassured him that residents received drug counselling and there was no need to worry. Brian also realized that sometimes staff 'rewarded' residents by leaving the front door open late at night, 'forgetting' to lock the fridge, or 'ignoring' the stack of alcohol pushed to the back of the shelves.

One of his 'key-worker' residents confided in him that the residents were planning a 'birthday bash with presents for everyone'. Brian suspected that other staff would have been told the same thing. As no one mentioned the plans he was afraid that saying something might break the boundary of trust if he had been told 'in confidence'.

Brian was on leave the weekend of the 'bash', and returned to find a silent, deserted building. The residents' rooms stood empty and the staff sat despondently in the TV lounge. The party had gone horribly wrong. Drugs and alcohol had unleashed a flood of pent-up emotion that the locked doors could not contain. All the residents had been asked to leave the hostel. The exclusions were not necessarily permanent. The staff promised to reconsider each person's situation individually.

Over the ensuing weeks Brian was part of a series of 'debriefing' meetings arranged with an external consultant to assist the staff group in understanding what had happened. The members of the group realized that they had worked within an unconscious assumption that because they controlled the physical boundaries of the hostel they also contained the emotions of the residents. This overlooked the true reality of the situation. The staff had received no supervision for their work: there had been an assumption that because they were young they would understand the, mostly young, residents. Therefore, the staff had been unaware of their own contribution to the 'cocktail' of emotions. One key issue was the degree to which the staff had projected their own adolescent need to challenge boundaries on to the residents, to avoid being like 'bad' parents. Being careless with keys and drugs colluded with the residents' desire to escape from reality by whatever means possible. Also, the staff group had not acknowledged their own need for acceptance by the residents.

The staff had established outer boundaries but had applied them so inconsistently that they reinforced the residents' view that boundaries are arbitrary and uncontaining. Had the staff been able to maintain boundaries consistently and fairly, the residents might have learned that thinking about painful feelings can be a way of controlling impulsive, destructive behaviours. This example illustrates how over-reliance on outer boundaries can mask the lack of strong inner boundaries.

A parochial church council

The departure of its vicar left a church, situated in a prosperous suburban area, without a leader. Considerable time elapsed before the post was advertised. During this time a sub-committee of the Parochial Church Council was set up to manage church affairs. The previous vicar had managed the church in a very boundaried, but democratic, style. Meetings had been held in the hall attached to the church. All Council members were involved in decision-making.

When the vicar left, the sub-committee took its position very seriously and assumed 'parental' responsibility for running of the church. However, they quickly began to resent the way their decisions were challenged by other parishioners who, in the sub-committee's eyes, were ungrateful. The boundaries within which the sub-committee originally functioned began to subtly shift. It was decided it would be much more comfortable to meet in each other's homes rather than in the church hall.

Over time, the sub-committee members began to lose their sense of accountability to the church congregation. Fewer and fewer of their decisions were referred back to the Parochial Church Council. The crunch finally came when the sub-committee decided to use funds raised by the summer fair to finance two of its members on a pilgrimage rather than to subsidise parishioners who wished to attend the summer camp, as was the usual practice. It seemed that enjoying the comfort of their own homes had isolated them from the reality of parishioners who were not as well off. Not surprisingly, the fair was not well attended and for the first time ran at a deficit.

A member of the Parochial Church Council approached the diocese asking for help to heal the split that had developed between the Council and the sub-committee. A meeting took place with a diocesan representative within the church hall, so all present were once again within the 'official' container. As the two groups challenged each other, what had happened gradually became understood. The sub-committee became aware of how they had retreated from the enormity of their task and the other Council members realized that they had left the responsibility for running the church with the sub-committee. Members were able to admit their grief at the loss of their vicar, an important aspect of their former containment. The return to the container (represented by the church hall and the diocesan representative) facilitated the return to the reality of working with the Bishop to find a new vicar – thus restoring the boundary around the congregation.

A home visit

John, a young volunteer from Victim Support, was sent to visit an elderly man, Frank. An intruder had broken into Frank's flat, threatened him, and run off with his money. John was greeted by the old man saying, 'You look a bit young. What use are you going to be?' Frank grabbed

John's identity card and inspected it with suspicion. He began a tirade against the caretaker of his apartment block, the police, the intruder, and the volunteer, who had 'taken his time to visit'. Ten minutes later they were still in the doorway. John knew he had to exercise sensitivity, but to be of help he also had to gain access to a private space. Despite feeling attacked himself, John realized that the old man was probably reliving the trauma of standing in his doorway, and not being able to stop the intruder pushing past into the flat.

John decided to tell Frank how long he would stay and that he felt it would be best if they spoke in the lounge where they could be comfortable. Once in the lounge, John suggested to Frank that he sit on the sofa. John sat on a chair at some distance from Frank in order to give him a sense of his own space. The television was on. John asked Frank whether it would be a good idea to turn it off so they could talk without distraction. Frank agreed. Then Frank was able to express his underlying distress, his shame at his vulnerability, and his fear of the intruder's return. John was able to listen and to make suggestions about improving the safety of his flat. He finished at the prearranged time and arranged to visit again.

In this case, the volunteer was sufficiently sensitized by his training and supervision to recognize the value of his countertransference response (his feeling of being attacked) in dealing with Frank's very real fear of his home boundary being broken into again. John gave him time on the doorstep to get accustomed to his presence and made clear his own boundaries (of time and space). Once within the flat, John was able to create a safe container around the interview by maintaining a respectful distance and by indicating his interest through careful listening.

A personal emergency while at work

A psychotherapist's son has broken his leg and she has to leave the clinic immediately. The secretary is asked to inform patients that their appointments have been cancelled. If the therapist does not wish her patients to be given personal details of why she is not available, the secretary will need to be informed of this. If at all possible, a brief discussion about what the secretary should say is not only courteous but an important aspect of maintaining the professional boundary. The therapist is likely to be aware that some patients will be upset, and if there is time, might communicate this to the secretary. The patients, and possibly also the secretary, will need an opportunity to talk with the therapist about the event at their next meeting.

Secretaries and receptionists are essential to the efficient running of hospital and GP clinics, and most medical support staff will be aware of the need for confidentiality, particularly with relations wanting information about patients. Because the boundaries around psychotherapeutic practice are unusual, and do not conform to societal norms, they might present a particular challenge to support staff. They might need help in managing the powerful feelings that such boundaries can arouse.

A GP surgery

Vanessa took up her counselling post within a GP's surgery with great enthusiasm. She had clear views about the importance of boundaries in counselling work, but was not prepared for the lack of boundaries having such an impact on her ability to work. This GP practice was situated within a regional Health Centre, but their catchment area was small, serving only those people registered with them. The counsellor quickly became aware of the rivalry that existed between Health Centre and GP staff in sharing inadequate space. The division of tasks and responsibility was also complicated. A district nurse and health visitor employed by the GP practice were based within the Health Centre, but the Health Centre also employed its own team of nurses. In some instances both Health Centre and GP practice nurses were offering the same services, e.g., baby clinics, antenatal clinics, and well-woman clinics.

It became apparent to Vanessa that meetings between Health Centre and GP practice staff designed to facilitate conflict resolution were being used to snipe at each other. An example occurred during a clinical meeting when the GP practice's district nurse reported on a course he had attended about treatments for sexual abuse. The Health Centre nursing manager interrupted to point out that since a member of *her* staff group had attended a similar course, his report was redundant. The district nurse asked for clarification on an aspect of the recommended treatment that he had not understood. The health centre nurse then admitted that she had left the course at lunchtime due to a migraine and had not heard the relevant information! Rather than talking about the lack of funding and space, both staff groups found reasons not to cooperate. Such an atmosphere made it impossible for useful information and sharing of resources to occur. When resources are scarce, resentment can easily be projected from one part of the organization to another.

Vanessa discovered she had not been allocated a room in which to see her clients. The GP practice manager explained that she could not have the same room each time. On one occasion Vanessa was using the room belonging to the dental suite. The dentist was not expected that day but, as Vanessa was soon to discover, appointments had been rescheduled to deal with a backlog. As usual, Vanessa put an 'Engaged' notice on the door to avoid intrusion and went to collect her client. As she returned to the room with her client, she was confronted by the dental clerk who explained that extra appointments had been arranged later that afternoon. During the course of the session the dentist herself walked in, but left when she realized the room was in use. Vanessa's client remarked, 'An apology wouldn't have gone amiss, just barging in like that.' A little later the session was again interrupted by the phone ringing. Ordinarily, Vanessa ignored the phone when with a client, but the dentist rushed in to take the call in case it was one of her patients. During the session the client remained sympathetic towards her struggling counsellor.

The following week Vanessa listened carefully for anything that might reflect the client's reaction to the previous week's incidents. She detected that the client did indeed feel some resentment that Vanessa had not protected the session from impingement. The client said it reminded her of her childhood when she felt her mother did not protect her from witnessing the domestic violence of the household. She had always wished her mother would leave her father and take the children with her. This association showed that the client had picked up the unconscious violence between members of staff in the previous week's intrusions. Such boundary violations are a frequent occurrence when there is a struggle for scarce resources.

The presence of a counsellor in a workplace, whether medical, educational, or industrial, can at times provoke rivalrous feelings among colleagues. Other staff might feel they have failed when a referral has to be made for more specialized treatment. There might be envy of the counsellor who can spend so much time with one individual or of the patient who receives so much attention. In response, the counsellor's work might be devalued in a number of ways, such as careless intrusion.

This example illustrates how rivalries and muddled boundaries can affect the whole ethos of the organization. This can be further complicated in medical settings where 'invasive' procedures on a patient's body (crossing physical boundaries) can encourage the practitioner to become insensitive to interpersonal boundaries.

Institutional defences

It is important that boundaries do not become so impermeable that they turn into barriers. Increasingly, working practice is governed by institutional and legal codes. Unfortunately, these sometimes have the opposite effect to what was intended. Rather than safeguarding, they can challenge the safe boundaries around work. A close examination of working practices often reveals a system of defences against the anxiety of work (Menzies Lyth, 1988). Institutions can unwittingly create a culture of 'us and them'. In part this is defensive, a means of dealing with the very real anxiety of working with stress and pain.

For example, the managers of a local hospital were under pressure to cut costs and decided to close down some wards without informing the medical staff. The pressure contributed to their anxiety to such an extent that they did not think about the effect on patients for whom beds would still have to be found. In hierarchical organizations where there are poor channels of communication, the same boundary that protects the professional from too much anxiety can, unfortunately, protect him from an awareness of the patient's anxieties. Patients whose worries are pushed away might become depressed, or might resentfully attack the boundaries that isolate them from the staff. When members of the local community became aware of the planned cuts, they angrily attacked members of the medical staff, who had themselves been kept in ignorance. A joint protest march on the hospital's management headquarters by members of the public and the medical staff turned into a violent confrontation. Only after the police were called did the management team offer a room in which to hold an emergency consultation meeting. Here, belatedly, they were able to agree a compromise.

If the boundaries between levels of staffing had been more permeable, earlier consultation might have prevented a difficult situation from developing into a crisis. How a workplace is constructed will affect the work that it is possible to do within it. Managers' appreciation of psychological boundaries can promote a sense of containment for the people working in an institution and help them to work more effectively. Unfortunately, some management cultures do not seem to understand that staff members are themselves within the container with the patients. They are more comfortable with a culture of 'us' (professionals) and 'them' (patients). This rigidity can lead to a lack of awareness of patients' anxieties.

Similarly, it is incumbent on senior staff to recognize the impact of painful work on the emotional life of their workers and to provide staff support and supervision where appropriate. When professional staff ignore, or fail to appreciate, the impact of this kind of work on their emotional life, tragedy can result. Unfortunately, it is not uncommon for people within the caring professions to seek relief from their feelings in drink, drugs, and, in extreme cases, suicide. A vital element of training, therefore, should be encouraging an awareness of the importance of containment in the workplace. Allowing space to think, providing safe clinical supervision (i.e., not provided by direct managers) either individually or in groups, and providing access to confidential staff counselling are the main elements of such containment.

Summary

These examples of work within different settings highlight the complexity of boundary issues outside the consulting room. The CPN had to manage a transition to a more boundaried relationship with her psychotherapy client. Brian, in the hostel for young homeless people, had to understand how he had become caught up in the ambivalent attitude of the staff group to maintaining secure boundaries. The church sub-committee and Parochial Church Council had to recognize the implications of their failure to maintain the container (the church itself) for their decision-making process. John, the Victim Support worker, had to negotiate boundaries within the client's own flat after the robbery.

Within any institution, or in premises shared with others, there is an additional dynamic – other people and their expectations. Vanessa, the GP counsellor, had to engage with the attitudes of professional colleagues, as well as coping with the client work itself.

CHAPTER SIX

CONFIDENTIALITY

The concepts of boundary and confidentiality are closely linked. Psychotherapy, counselling, and psychoanalysis are all based on the premise that the patient is free to say whatever is on his mind and the therapist is similarly free to think. It is a common assumption that the boundaries around a session are not only to do with time and space but also with an assurance that what is communicated between therapist and patient will largely stay in the room. Like the well-sealed vessel used by the alchemists, the confidential nature of therapeutic work is meant to provide a secure container in which difficult and sometimes volatile feelings can be exposed. The trust that develops over time is, to a large extent, encouraged by this sense of privacy.

Views on confidentiality differ within the therapeutic community. Some, like Christopher Bollas, a contemporary psychoanalyst, make the case for absolute confidentiality. Bollas (2003, p. 157) maintains that the psychoanalytic method of free association and evenly suspended attentiveness depends on free expression. Free expression is undermined if confidentiality is compromised in areas such as sexuality and violence (although it could be argued that all areas of personal pain might be similarly affected). The therapist needs to be able to 'listen freely' rather than to 'listen out' for information that would compel him to report the patient to the authorities. Bollas writes, 'We must argue that confidentiality is held by our profession – not by our patients – so that we may discuss our patients with colleagues, clear in our minds that in so doing we are not referring our patients to the criminal justice system' (*ibid.*, p. 173).

On the other hand, Dr Richard Lucas, a psychiatrist and psychoanalyst, (Lucas, 2002, p. 2) argues for a balance between the rights of the individual and the needs of society. 'Normally, one would expect that patient confidentiality would be preserved at all times, in relation to analytic therapy. Potentially dangerous situations are far more likely to arise over inappropriate maintaining of confidentiality.' In other words, there are occasions when not 'reporting' can lead to patients being a risk to themselves and others; patients who deny or rationalize their illness pose a particular problem for the therapist. In these cases it is essential for them to be able to talk openly with the psychiatrist, GP, and responsible relations.

'The right to confidence is based on the idea that the information belongs to the person who imparted it – rather as though it was a piece of property' (Layton, 2003, p. 151). The legal implication of this is that the information contained in a therapist's notes belongs to the patient. If a patient wants to see or disclose the notes, the therapist is obliged to hand them over. However, this contrasts with the opinion offered by the BCP [now BPC] Working Group on Confidentiality in the concluding article of the same journal that featured Layton's paper: 'Assured and predictable neutrality and confidentiality are absolutely central to psychoanalytic psychotherapy and psychoanalysis without which the existence of these as available treatments is seriously compromised for all patients; and some practitioners would say it is impossible to practise' (BCP, 2003, pp. 193–194).

Limitations

Many factors in the social, legal, and institutional context of therapy constrain the impermeability of the confidential framework; confidentiality is not the same as secrecy.

When a patient reveals serious intent to commit suicide, information about having committed a crime, or evidence of paedophilia, confidentiality is immediately challenged. Questions about safeguarding the patient, the therapist, and the public will all need to be considered.

In private practice, it might be necessary to inform the patient's GP when there are changes in his emotional state that could require a change of medication or hospital admission. Within an institution where a patient is seen by a number of different professionals, communication between them is often necessary. For example, a therapist working with a schizophrenic patient might notice increasing evidence of disturbed sleep patterns and delusional thoughts. It is part of the therapist's duty of care to inform the patient's psychiatrist. Therapists working with recovering substance abusers might need to tell relevant team members if the patient begins 'to use' again. Here, the therapist is part of a team and as such must function within the treatment network. However, the therapist should bear in mind that the patient is also part of the team involved in his care. The patient should be consulted when the therapist is considering contacting another professional involved in his care. But, ultimately, the therapist has a duty of care to ensure the safety of the patient, so information about potentially harmful changes in behaviour might have to be disclosed even against a patient's wishes.

Clinical examples

1. A teacher of previous blameless record is unable to resist escalating sexual contact with young adolescent pupils in his school. Prosecutable behaviour has already occurred, but is not yet public. He knows he is in need of help, but is not sure where to seek it. He would be 'safe' in going to his priest, as he could legally maintain absolute confidentiality. But a doctor or psychotherapist would be bound by the GMC guidelines and the *Children Act* (1989) to contact Social Services. The therapist who continues to work with the patient might put others at risk in not informing the authorities. On the other hand, the therapist who reports the incident is likely to lose the patient and the possibility of helping him in the longer term.

2. A young psychiatrist in training reported to his psychoanalyst that he was aware of paedophilic desires. He did not say whether he intended to act on his feelings. With the agreement of the patient, the analyst stopped the analysis but offered once-weekly supportive therapy. He did not report the patient to the authorities and the patient remained in the training. Subsequently, the psychiatrist abused a ten-year-old boy. Ten years later, when the boy was twenty-one years old, the analyst was sued for not doing more to protect the child. The analyst was found guilty of negligence for not informing the college authorities at the time about his patient.

3. A twenty-year-old history student who lived alone was brought to the Emergency Department by neighbours after an attempted suicide. A provisional diagnosis of acute schizo-affective disorder was made by the duty doctor, and, after a brief admission, home treatment was

agreed as a safe alternative. Although at that time the patient was not in a sufficiently lucid state of mind to give consent to her family being contacted, the Community Mental Health Team invited her parents, who lived abroad, to come to London to meet with them.

Over time, it became clear that this breaking of confidentiality had particular significance. The patient had been attempting to gain independence from her parents' controlling ambitions for her, and she felt that this had now been undermined. She believed that her own academic interests had always been undervalued by her parents, who regarded financial success as all-important. At college, she had been very successful in her course work and slowly began to make friends, but this success was itself stressful for her because of her fear of high expectations.

Although it seemed ethically 'right' to have broken her confidentiality and included her family, it was experienced by the patient as a repeat of her parents' controlling behaviour. Ideally, the need for confidentiality has to be balanced against the need to help the individual concerned as appropriately as possible. How that balance is reached in each case is rarely straightforward.

4. A young man was referred for therapy to deal with relationship problems. He had experienced an emotionally and physically deprived childhood. The parents were emotionally distant and had to work long hours to support a large family. It gradually emerged that there had been a terrible tragedy in the family history. A close relation who was mentally unstable had fatally wounded another family member. This was a secret shared but not talked about by the immediate and extended family.

The patient had succeeded professionally and had a financially rewarding but demanding job, which involved high profile deals. The therapist, impressed by the importance of the patient's job, agreed to see him later than usual because of his long work hours.

Despite the therapist's impression of an enviably rewarding job, the patient soon began to complain about unhappiness at work and a feeling that he was being bullied. He decided to undertake further training to try to secure an even better job. Preoccupied with whether he would 'measure up', he spoke of wanting to leave therapy in order to fulfil the demands of his course. The therapist therefore assumed they were working towards an ending.

The patient's situation at work started to deteriorate rapidly. Suddenly he went to his GP and secured a sick note for stress. He immediately sought legal advice in order to make an official complaint to the Employment Tribunal because of 'unfair treatment' at work. The GP telephoned the therapist. There was a shared concern about the emotional impact of an adversarial legal system on their patient's fragile mental state. Following this conversation, the therapist wrote to the GP to confirm their discussion.

Without any warning, the therapist received a written request for the clinical notes from the patient's legal team. On discussion, at his next session, the patient told him that he believed the clinical notes would provide useful evidence of his mistreatment at work. The therapist believed that this was unlikely, because his notes were mostly concerned with the interaction between himself and the patient, and his countertransference responses, not information about the work situation. He wrote back refusing to pass on the notes on the grounds of confidentiality. He explained that disclosure could be harmful to the patient's well-being, and the notes, written for the therapist's own use, were unlikely to make sense to anyone else.

Unknown to the therapist, the GP's medical notes had also been requested by the patient's legal team, and the GP had released them. The medical notes included the letter sent by the therapist. On the basis of this letter, the patient's legal team renewed their efforts to obtain the therapist's notes. By this time, the patient's Tribunal case for compensation had begun, and his claim was being opposed by his employer. The patient's lawyer wrote again, explaining that the employer's solicitors were now also pressing for the notes to be produced. They explained that a court-appointed psychiatrist was compiling a report on the patient's mental state and that the therapist's notes would provide evidence of the patient's state of mind at the time of the work problems.

Being unfamiliar with the legal system, the therapist felt increasingly anxious and intimidated. As pressure to release the notes increased, he realized that something was being acted out that probably belonged in the therapy. However, it was difficult to work on this because the therapy itself was now in a confusing state. The compensation claim absorbed all of the patient's interest; he no longer mentioned leaving but did not seem to be interested in the therapist's efforts to link his anger with the employer to himself or his parents. Ashamed about being in such a muddle, the therapist tried to deal with the pressure alone rather than seek the advice of colleagues. Feeling bullied, he decided again to refuse to release the notes.

Suddenly, one Monday morning, the therapist was ordered to attend the Employment Tribunal Hearing in two days' time with his patient and the legal team. The therapist was told that he would be asked to defend his decision not to provide the notes, and was advised to bring his own legal representation because he might be personally liable for costs in excess of £40,000 if he lost. At last, the therapist contacted his professional organization for advice, and was referred to a solicitor who explained that the therapist had no case because the patient himself did not object to his notes being handed over. She reassured the therapist that the patient's confidentiality would be preserved because the notes would be seen only by the court-appointed psychiatrist. She added that the Tribunal's primary duty is to the interests of justice: 'inconvenience, embarrassment or other difficulties caused to a witness are less important. It is up to the tribunal to decide whether or not the notes are relevant, not the therapist.'

Feeling humiliated and violated, the therapist released his notes with the stipulation that they be seen only by the psychiatrist. He did not attend the Tribunal. The patient came to his next session very angry with the therapist. He had seen the notes because copies of them had, in fact, been distributed to everyone present at the Tribunal, including the patient himself. He had lost his case and blamed the therapist. He left the session early and did not return.

Without adequate supervision or self-reflection, the therapist had become caught up in a painful re-enactment of the patient's family situation. It would appear that the therapist was over-impressed by the client's high-profile job. From the very beginning this affected his usual boundary setting, leading him to offer an appointment time outside his ordinary working hours. No doubt he was also unconsciously influenced by a desire to be a 'better parent', one who could be expansive with time. Despite giving the client adequate time, the therapist could not counter the patient's fear of his anger, the ingrained ethos of family secrecy, and his own envy of his patient's high-profile life. This combination of factors probably made it impossible for secret feelings to do with anger and revenge to be dealt with confidentially in the consulting room. Instead, the client projected his anger with his parents on to his employers and then expected his therapist to use his confidential notes to assist the Tribunal attack on the employers. Unconsciously, of course, he was attacking the ability of the therapist and the therapeutic relationship to help him – in effect re-enacting the original family murder. It was as if he were saying, 'the consulting room is not a high-profile enough place to reveal the family secret (the employer/parent 'bullying'). I must find a more suitable place'. Sadly, this case is a good example of how being bullied can lead to the victim himself becoming the bully. The client ended up bullying the therapist into court and destroying his own potential lifeline. Interestingly, in exposing the situation in a court setting, he also put his own behaviour 'in the dock'. Had there been adequate supervision and the therapist more aware of his own feelings, at an earlier stage, the collusion between his and his client's over-valuing of the high-profile life might have been averted and the outcome been very different.

CHAPTER SEVEN

PROFESSIONAL BOUNDARIES AND CONTAINMENT

Introduction

Given the nature of the experience in the consulting room, it is not surprising that the 'therapeutic couple', the therapist and client, need reliable support and containment. The consulting room and the space around it form a part of their immediate physical boundary. An ethos of confidentiality forms a less tangible, but equally important, boundary. Beyond this, one could imagine a series of concentric circles that, like the layers of an onion, define and encircle the therapeutic experience. The outermost layers, farthest from the consulting room, are the legal constraints, government mandates, and cultural expectations of society. These enclose other layers represented by professional registration bodies as well as the Codes of Ethics and guidelines of the training body. Within the layer framed by the therapist's training is the containment of the therapist's own therapy and supervision, the theoretical model(s), and the therapist's belief system. In situations where the work takes place outside the therapist's own consulting room, the constraints of the institution form yet another layer of containment. Even the way the therapist makes use of her mind and understands her role become significant aspects of containment around the therapy. Of course any of these layers can, at times, represent a lack of containment.

Legal constraints

The cases described in the previous chapter illustrate the impact of the law on the therapeutic process. In 'Confidentiality' case example 4 (see pp. 77–81), the boundaries around therapy were challenged by the court in its request for information contained in the patient's notes. Fortunately, this is relatively uncommon, but when it does happen there is a real danger that the information gleaned from session notes might be used to the disadvantage of the patient. Disclosure can be detrimental to his mental health and can bring the therapeutic relationship to an end. Although legally a therapist can ask that disclosure be limited to particular parties (e.g., the court-appointed psychiatrist), the court can decide to release the notes to everyone involved. In reality, it appears that each case is fought on a case by case basis. The therapist in this position needs to consult with colleagues, the training organization, and probably legal advisers. The acts concerned are the *Data Protection Act* (1998), the *Human Rights Act* (1998) and the *Access to Health Records Act* (1990).

In the case of paedophilia, the relevant law is the *Children Act* (1989). Unfortunately, these laws are both comprehensive and vague.

Codes of Ethics

In therapy things can, and sometimes do, go wrong. Jung (1946, par. 364–365) writes extensively of the dangers of 'psychic infection'; by this he means the therapist, because of his emotional proximity to the patient, is in danger of being infected by his feelings. 'Psychic infection' is what allows the therapist to experience the client's feelings within himself (the countertransference). Although an understanding of the countertransference can lead to therapeutic change, Jung warned that it is not easy for the therapist to become aware of what is happening and there is always a danger of the therapist taking action rather than thinking and, hopefully, interpreting. Jung recognized this problem and was the first to 'demand that anybody who intends to practise psychotherapy should first submit to a training analysis, yet even the best preparation will not suffice to teach him everything about the unconscious' (*ibid.* par. 366).

Each training organization currently recognized as a member of either the United Kingdom Council for Psychotherapy (UKCP) or the British Psychoanalytic Council (BPC, formerly British Confederation for Psychotherapists, or BCP) must implement a Code of Ethics that delineates behaviour which is unprofessional. The areas covered by Codes of Ethics include: the prohibition against sexual or financial exploitation of patients and supervisees, the obligation to maintain patient confidentiality, fraudulent claims about qualifications, etc. Codes of Ethics are generally available to the public upon request.

Sometimes a process meant to address and understand the needs of the patient becomes one that is more concerned to protect the therapist. Gabbard and Lester, experts in boundary violations in psychotherapy, evaluated and treated more than seventy cases of therapists who had sexual relationships with their patients (Gabbard &

Lester, 1995). Gabbard's suggestions for attempting to prevent this include ongoing supervision, education on ethics as part of training, more rigorous training analysis/therapy, and consideration of the therapist's level of satisfaction outside of work. However, total prevention is unrealistic, even where a trainee's therapist is required to report to the training committee (Sandler, 2004).

Complaints and appeals' procedures

Ethics complaints have traditionally been handled by a committee of members from within the organizations themselves. This practice is gradually changing to that of a regulation committee including lay members and operating outside each individual organization.

Ethics committees have the power to investigate complaints and, in minor cases, to provide an opportunity for conciliation. When a major complaint is upheld, sanctions can be recommended. The therapist concerned might be asked to have further therapy or supervision or, in the most severe cases, might be suspended from practice or expelled from the organization.

Codes of practice or practice guidelines

Codes of practice differ from Codes of Ethics. They are recommendations about best practice in support of the regulatory boundaries contained in the Codes of Ethics. They cover issues such as the necessity to make clear the contractual expectations of the practitioner before therapy begins (e.g., charging fees for missed sessions), the responsibility to appoint professional executors who can act on a member's behalf in the event of sudden incapacity or death, the requirement for practitioners to undertake regular continuing professional development, including supervision, and guidelines for liaison with GPs and other mental health professionals involved with the patient.

Most Codes of Ethics expect the professional to refrain from claiming to possess qualifications he does not possess, and from practising beyond the limitations of his training. The clear intention is that the work done should correspond to the training and experience of the individual therapist. Yet it is not uncommon to find patients continuing in long-term non-intensive work who might never improve without more specialized or intensive help. Of course, they might not come to any harm, but they could get bored or discouraged and eventually stop. Problems can develop later when they need further help but might dismiss counselling or psychotherapy because it has already been tried. Had the original therapist recognized that the patient needed a different kind of help, he could have been referred on and perhaps have continued to develop.

Issues of differentiation

In addition to the cultural pressure against differentiation spoken of in Chapter 3 there is confusion about how to value different kinds of therapeutic work. Because the words 'psychotherapist' and 'psychotherapy' might for some have a higher status than 'counsellor' and 'counselling', there can be a strong pull towards using these terms loosely, if not inappropriately. Slippage in word usage occurs because, understandably, the practitioner wants the work to be valued. However, this tendency could be seen as an aspect of magical thinking – using a word to create what the practitioner wants to be rather than becoming what he wants to be through further training or belief in his own distinctive work as something of equal value. It would be similar to a farmer who wishes to paint declaring that he is a painter rather than a farmer who paints pictures. It is interesting that the public itself appears to use the term 'counselling' more often than 'psychotherapy'. This might be in order to demystify the work and/or because this label somehow feels less frightening.

The more we value the distinctiveness of what each practitioner brings to therapeutic work, the less often do terms such as 'psychotherapy' have to be used in an indiscriminate manner to confer value or status. It is to be hoped that the practitioner's realistic belief in his capacities is, in the end, what confers value on his work. Paradoxically, the use of the term 'psychotherapy' in an overly inclusive way actually devalues counselling and other forms of intervention, for it implies that these disciplines cannot stand under their own rubric and that there is not sufficient meaning in their own distinctiveness. To acquire value they have to assume someone else's label. Forthcoming statutory regulation of the profession may, in any case, provide limitations around such fluid use of terms.

The confusion in the valuation of therapeutic work is often augmented by a confusion of terminology. Grammatically, we confuse *who* is doing the work (the psychotherapist) with *what* is being done (the psychotherapy) and both of these with *how* it is being done (psychotherapeutically). Although it is accurate to say that different professionals are all working psychotherapeutically, they are not necessarily doing the same kind of psychotherapy work nor are they all necessarily psychotherapists. Equally, various professionals might all be practising psychotherapy (in a variety of forms), but they are not necessarily all psychotherapists. It seems that *doing* psychotherapy slips all too easily into *being* a psychotherapist.

An interesting example of this came in the form of a flyer advertising the work of a local counsellor. Her own training was as a counsellor, but because the name of her training organization included the words counselling *and* psychotherapy, her own work was described as counselling *and* psychotherapy. Not only was this confusing, it was also clearly misleading. She was promoting work for which she was not trained and this, according to most Codes of Ethics, is unethical.

Clinical example

A recently-qualified counsellor brought a new client for supervision. The client had found her name through a website and had conveyed a sense of urgency and desperation, even on the telephone. The first meeting was filled with a pressured and emotional description of the client's anguish, and the counsellor had found it difficult to get a word in edgeways. Towards the end of that meeting, the counsellor interrupted to suggest that they talk about practicalities, such as the possible timing of a regular session. The client unexpectedly revealed that she was expecting to come three times weekly, because 'that's what psychotherapy is, and that's what I want'.

The counsellor was taken aback; she had been trained to see clients once-weekly, but realized that she was listed on the website under the category of 'Counselling and psychotherapy'. Without thinking it through, she had gone along with the client's assumptions and expectations, seeing her for a second and third session during the same week before coming to supervision. She presented her experience of becoming overwhelmed by the client's material, which included some quite paranoid ideas about her neighbours having drilled an observation hole in the party wall. When the counsellor had linked the client's anxiety to the forthcoming weekend break, the client suddenly looked at her in a suspicious way and asked if she was a 'mind-reader'.

Supervision highlighted the counsellor's lack of experience with frequent sessions. They considered how the ethical issue of the counsellor not having been straight with the client about her level of skills had resulted in a clinical dilemma: how to proceed in the best interests of the client. It was agreed that the counsellor would give the client the choice of continuing with her once a week, or going to someone else for more frequent therapy.

Another strand of the complex issue of differentiation is the theoretical underpinning of therapeutic work. Psychodynamic work in all its variations—counselling, psychotherapy, and analysis – is supported by a body of theoretical knowledge. Although in many cases the work of these practitioners is very different, the same theory tends to be used by all. Of course, this makes some sense, because the person being helped is the same even if the practitioner is different and has different training. In addition, it is important to understand the dynamics of the psyche even if that knowledge is not used directly in the work. On the other hand, the use of common texts can be confusing and lead the practitioner unwittingly to have expectations of himself for which his training has not equipped him. A clinical example of a patient in three times weekly psychotherapy might be interesting to read but, as is clear from the above example, the pace and nature of the work would be very different from a client who attends counselling once a week or a patient who attends a psychiatric appointment even less often. It is important to match the content and manner in which interpretations are made with the intensity and spacing of sessions. A comment made about a patient's vulnerability might be tolerable if he is returning the next day and can clarify or protest against its meaning. The same comment made to the same patient who is not seen again for a week could be devastating. He might have been hurt, but cannot clarify what was meant for a week. His thoughts might build up and become persecutory; he could be filled with uncontainable anxiety. The practitioner who uses a variety of theoretical texts must be clear in his mind how he is using them, with whom, and in what context.

CHAPTER EIGHT

ENDING

Directly or indirectly, endings take one back to the beginning, back to why the client came in the first place and to what has happened between therapist and client since that time.

The difference between ending and stopping

One of the central issues in finishing the work is the difference between ending and stopping. Ending is a process. Stopping is just that – stopping. Ending involves a planned interaction between two people over time. Stopping does not. In between are the grey areas – an ending process agreed but, consciously or unconsciously, sabotaged. Having allowed time to draw things to a close, space for saying good-bye, reflection, or mourning, the client may simply not come, or, even more difficult, might arrive ten minutes before the end of the last session! For whatever reason, he cannot face the process involved in ending; instead, he has chosen to stop. From the counsellor's point of view, he leaves her to do the work of ending by herself, and that is not easy. She has to let go of the client in his absence and deal with all the feelings of being left in this manner, of the work being incomplete. Just as an unmourned child can affect the parents' relationship to the next sibling, so an unresolved ending with the counsellor might affect her relationship to the next client.

In those cases where the client insists on stopping and thereby eliminating the ending process, it is useful to ask oneself and to consider with the client (if he is still there) why he needs to do so. What is it that he fears in this ending space to such an extent that he needs it *not* to happen? The answer will almost certainly contain material vital to the continuation of the work and thereby to the client's further understanding. Whatever is in the answer might contain the essence of his psychic blockage not only now, but for years prior to arriving in the consulting room. In addition, the material in the blockage, if it *can* be considered, will contain the potential for further development of the work either in an extension of the current work, with someone else when a referral is being made, or, should he decide to finish at this stage, maybe within the client's own development. Of course, sometimes a patient reappears later on to face what could not be faced earlier.

Clinical example

The client who stops rather than ends will have all sorts of means, conscious and unconscious, at his disposal to ensure that it happens in just that way. He might arrive for the last ten minutes of the last session, as we have suggested. The therapist might think, 'Ten minutes is ten minutes, quite a lot can happen in that time.' This is true, but if he is determined to stop rather than to end, he might have enlisted further support for his intention. This will be the occasion when his wife will have had to attend her ailing mother and have left the two-year-old behind with him. The two-year-old might have been brought along to the session or be in the car outside. Now the therapist is left with ten minutes in which to end and a much more complex situation – does she consider the immediate danger to the two-year-old left outside in the car, the two-year-old behaviour of the client putting her in an impossible position, or the two-year-old in herself, who might want to scream in rage and say it's all too much; how could she be expected to cope in such circumstances. Oh, and we forgot to mention, because he has not been to his sessions for some weeks, there is also an unpaid account to be presented and paid within this time! He will probably face the therapist with the two-year-old assertion that as he was not here for the sessions he should not have to pay for them.

One way of deciphering this scene is to speculate about the common element – the two-year-old. This might have been a difficult time for this young man, when he was, in actuality, two. Perhaps he was blocked at that age, metaphorically left outside in the car or dragged along when mother was preoccupied with other events in her life. Maybe something happened to him at that age which was not an ending with due notice, but something that stopped abruptly – a significant person dying without warning, an important carer who left without saying good-bye. It is as if he is bringing this reality into the consulting room in a manner which reflects how it happened then – without warning and with no space to do anything about it. Perhaps there were too many needs of too many people to be considered in the emotional equivalent of ten minutes. And, of course, two-year-olds pay for the time and space they take up, so from the two-year-old perspective a final account feels irrelevant!

Sometimes the two-year-old aspect of the client can be rescued at the last minute by a somewhat older internal figure (perhaps a more trusting self developed during a previous phase of work together assisted by the therapist's judicious use of interpretation). If not, the therapist will need to deal with her own feelings about the work being left in this manner and to have done some thinking about what feelings were being enacted by the client. It could be just the therapist's luck that he will turn up punctually the next week at his old time and be totally baffled that a new client is being shown into the room in his space! This could be another clue. Maybe the precipitate ending all those years ago had to do with a sibling that had arrived 'without notice', a sibling whom all these years later he was compelled to revisit.

Of course, this is an example of someone who could not face the ending because of the opportunity it would have provided for reliving the pain of what was blocking him. In contrast, a different person might have been able to use a period of ending to face some of this upset. This might have been the basis for consolidating the work with him, extending the contract to work on new areas, or referring him on for psychotherapy or even analysis with the expectation that the experiences of loss beginning to emerge in the ending process could be given further space. In any case, this is a good example of how the process of ending, or indeed even the attempt to avoid having an ending, can throw into the arena quite new material that has not been accessible earlier in the work. It is as if our imagined client believes that the counsellor will become, for example, the mother who actually deserted him so long ago. To some extent, of course, this is true. Space given to the ending can provide a forum for experiencing feelings of loss about the ending of the work together and this could connect with other experiences of unresolved loss in the past. It could be that the client has an accurate sense of his own limitations in this regard. Experiencing the loss of the counsellor and other unresolved losses might actually be too much for him, given his immature ego development and the possibility that the work will not be continuing. Equally, the client might have developed quite a shrewd intuition over years of dealing with vulnerable caretakers and be able to judge that the present counsellor could not cope with the level of his distress that would be evoked.

But isn't it interesting or ironic that, in attempting to avoid the pain of an ending, our client actually comes back the following week, as if to retrieve unconsciously what he had been so determined to leave out, his loss and pain. One could understand it both as a repetition compulsion, meeting without warning the new 'client/sibling', and as an attempt, albeit an awkward one, to retrieve the space he so adamantly insisted he did not need. The central point here is that ending contains a process essential to the work and raises issues for both the client and the counsellor which might not be revealed until that ending process begins. Thus, it is a paradox of the work that some of the most painful material might come at a time when the end is in sight, just when the client begins to imagine life without the support of the therapeutic encounter. It is no surprise that an ending might be strongly resisted.

The practical aspects of ending

The final account

Stopping or ending therapy involves both emotional and practical aspects. An important practical issue is the final account and the question of when to present it. If it is left to the last session to be consistent with a pattern of giving it at the end of the month, it might be forgotten by either counsellor or client. Alternatively, it can be given one or several sessions before the end. This introduces a change of pattern, but maybe one that helps to signal in a concrete manner that the overall pattern of sessions is about to change. The timing of the account itself might form a part of the discussion of the ending and might raise feelings about it. These might focus around the fact that this *is* the final account and how it feels not to be having another in the future, indeed not to be in this relationship in the future.

The timing of the ending

A practical and emotional aspect of ending is its actual timing – when to do it. In some of the shorter-term forms of the work, and especially where a service provider is involved, the end might be prescribed from the beginning. There might be a maximum number of sessions provided, and both counsellor and client are restricted by this external definition of need. In other situations, there might be a shortage of resources and what there is, is divided into small portions. When need is defined in a manner that does not coincide with professional judgement it can raise an ethical dilemma. In some cases, the counsellor might feel strongly enough about the client's need for continued therapy to consider referral elsewhere so that a compromise does not have to be made.

In other instances, the timing is prescribed at the beginning, not by an outside body or the institution, but by the client himself. This might be for reasons of finance, practical factors such as moving house or job, or a need to contain the experience for fear of being overwhelmed by it. Of course, there is often a subtle and complex

interaction between the concrete and emotional reasons
for ending. Nevertheless, in these instances, the ending is
fixed from the beginning. One enters the encounter with
the end already in mind.

This is a very different pattern from the open-ended
one, whether short-term or long-term. The open-ended
situation leaves the when, how, and why of the ending to
be decided. In some cases, this could mean that the timing
of the ending can be more closely related to therapeutic
need. In others, it means it is different from the fixed
ending, but presents other complications. First of all, how
does one know when to end when it has not been
prescribed? Sometimes, although the client is working in
an open-ended context, he has come with a specific goal
in mind. 'I want to sort out what to do about . . .' When
he gets to this point, he has a sense of having reached a
decision and he stops. There is a more or less clear time
to do so. Sometimes, he stops not because he has reached
a decision, but because he discovers in the course of the
work that the original dilemma could not be addressed in
such concrete terms. There was not an answer to be
found, but a process to go through whose value lay in
discovering that there *was not* an answer as such. There is
yet another possibility. The original search, whether or not
it leads to a resolution, puts the client in touch with a
desire to take the exploration further. It might be that the
original more limited search was his means of testing the
water and of discovering that it was safe to proceed, but
from now on in a less focused manner.

Having continued in an open-ended manner, how does
one know when to end? Generally speaking, it gradually
becomes apparent that change is occurring and this signals
a time to end. So, directly or indirectly, it comes into the

material. Outside interests – people, events, or activities – begin to take greater precedence. We will discuss the defensive use of these outside interests later, but here we are referring to a natural refocusing of energy, no doubt as a result of some of the work that has been done. Other signs of beginning to move towards an ending can be that the counsellor is not needed so frequently to sort out conflicts or feelings. The process is beginning to happen without the counsellor, between sessions. Increasingly, the client comes to report the problems he has successfully resolved rather than the problems he cannot solve alone.

In an ideal situation, where the therapist has choice over the timing of the ending, how much time does she allocate to the process? In our experience, there are two quite different patterns – one in which it feels possible for client and counsellor to designate a suitable time for ending and one in which the answer only emerges as the process of ending proceeds. Which pattern occurs in any particular situation will depend on the individual, the nature of the work so far, and the kinds of unresolved issues that the ending will inevitably produce. Most psychodynamic work is based on an assumption that the ending contains a process essential to the work and raises issues that might not be revealed until that ending process begins. This is what makes it so difficult to know how much time to allocate to the ending. In facing the ending, the therapeutic couple are on virgin territory. The therapist has never ended with this particular patient, so is not sure what to expect. The patient has not yet ended, so he also does not know what to expect. Using a geographical analogy, how does one plan a given amount of time for a journey when it is not known what that journey will entail or where the destination will be?

Clinical examples

A patient with a powerful memory of a traumatic leave-taking early in life wants to set a date far in advance, as if expecting an equally traumatic experience. In fact, because of work over a number of years in relation to the pain of holiday breaks, the trauma does not occur as expected. By the time the end does arrive, she is in touch with a gradually evolving empowerment, a sense that she carries something of lasting value inside her from the therapy.

On the other hand, another patient whose parent left him so early that he could not consciously recognise the 'parting', cannot imagine there being enough to deal with in more than a few weeks of ending, despite the value he has placed on the therapy. In the event, the patient experiences strong feelings of depression and fear of rejection as he becomes aware of the therapist's reluctant agreement to an overly short ending. The patient had defended against his feelings of being left until the end was under way and he could no longer 'not know' about them. It was as if he had at last been able 'to see' the absent parent leaving and re-experience at first hand what that earlier departure had meant. He was forced to acknowledge the power of his feelings and adjust the time of the ending to reflect more realistically what he was going through in relation to leaving the therapy.

The meaning of stopping or ending prematurely

The previous two clinical examples illustrated two quite different ways of finding the 'right' kind of space in which to end. Quite often, however, it seems that the client feels a need to stop or end in a way that the therapist considers premature. This section is a series of mini-vignettes giving some of the most common situations. Most practitioners will be able to put flesh and bones on these examples from their own experience with patients, or maybe from their own therapy. However, before we proceed, it is important to point out that many of the same remarks, if said in a different, non-defensive manner, could convey a different meaning. As is so often the case in therapy, it is the intent behind the words that is as important as the words themselves.

'We're not really getting anywhere'

This, of course, could be an accurate statement of a mutually frustrating stalemate. But think for a moment of one kind of stalemate – a state of paralysing fear. A patient might have proceeded without too much difficulty for the first six months of counselling. After a while, the work hits a plateau during which little new material is offered and an element of 'dullness' permeates the encounter. That kind of statement might be used by the patient as an indication that it is time to end. It is quite easy to collude with the patient's wish in an attempt to value what she has done so far, or perhaps not to be hurt oneself by the implied criticism. However, thinking back to Jung's theory of the opposites and applying it here, the therapist could speculate that it is not that the patient is getting nowhere, but the very opposite – that she is in fact getting *somewhere* and it is the expectation of this 'somewhere' that is paralysing. The stalemate in the work might be the patient's intuitive sense that the work is nearing unfamiliar, potentially difficult areas and she is afraid of continuing. So, in this instance, stopping or ending is in the interests of maintaining equilibrium. Being alert to the opposites can help to open up such a discussion.

'I have better things to do with my time, money, etc'

Again, this could be an indication of good reality testing, an indication that it is indeed time to move on. But said in a certain manner and with a denigrating tone, the therapist might be less than convinced. From the patient's point of view, it could be a justifiable retaliation, though perhaps not conscious. He could feel, 'You are taking my time and money and using it for your own ends. I have had enough of this; I will take my time and money and use it elsewhere, therefore depriving you of resources just as you attempt to deprive me.' Or, 'I am envious of what I see you getting. You don't appear to value me for my own sake, so I will take my resources elsewhere or use them for myself.' How much can be brought into the open will depend on the intensity of the work being done and on how able the patient is to acknowledge such negative feelings. But when the patient is able to use the opportunity to explore such feelings and the counsellor/therapist is able to face hearing them, there might no longer be a need to force an ending. In fact, having had the space to consider his reservations about the therapist, he might feel that the therapy is now worth the money he was previously reluctant to spend. Although the therapist and patient might not have recognized it at the time, he might have been saying, 'Can you help me find a way of making this encounter more valuable?' The value lay in the encounter that it was possible to have about his feelings. The patient was, in fact, correct. He was not getting value for money because he could not use the therapy to be open with his feelings!

'This just makes me more depressed. I felt happier before I came than now'

There are some people for whom psychodynamic counselling or therapy is not the appropriate choice. It does make them more depressed in a way that they cannot seem to use. But here we are considering the person who *can* make use of the therapeutic setting, but is finding it difficult at this particular time. It is important to recognize that the first part of this statement – 'This just makes me more depressed' – might be an accurate assessment of the client's experience. The person who has coped with life by denying his feelings might find endings in particular a challenge. If he has learned to cope in this manner, beginning to explore feelings that have been put aside for years can indeed make him depressed. To the general public or the person who has recently started therapy it can seem a nonsense coming to therapy and as a consequence getting more depressed, but this can be the case. It seems ironic that a complaint made to justify stopping or ending might in fact be an indication that things *are* happening; that it is worth pursuing the course because feelings are being stirred up inside and the patient who formerly cut off from his depression is now aware of it. But, of course, this is not comfortable. And this might be what the patient is saying in pointing out that he is more depressed. He is pointing to the pain he is experiencing – wanting help with it or wanting the therapist to know how much it hurts and what he is having to endure.

Although his words sound like a simple desire to stop, they might be a way into the experience of committing himself to therapy. He might be asking the therapist in the only way he can to *engage* with him over the struggle, *not to stop* doing so.

'I have a new job/baby/boss/position/house/wife/ girlfriend, etc. so I really have no choice about having to stop therapy'

We have put these numerous possibilities together because, viewed from the perspective we are taking in this section, they can all be viewed as ways of acting out – not the action in itself, but the accompanying drive to sabotage the therapy (often largely unconscious). In such cases, the therapist is often handed the situation after the fact – the job has been sought and accepted, the marriage arranged, the house sale completed. In other situations, where behaviour is more conscious, or at least potentially more conscious, the intention or plans might be brought to therapy at an earlier stage. The 'I have no choice' part of the statement is probably an indication of its unconsciousness and its 'drivenness'. It is also accurate in the sense that the patient is in the grip of such powerful forces within the experience of his therapy that he finds himself in a desperate need to leave.

Oedipal conflicts, if experienced too intensely, can lead the patient to seek a premature ending. Oedipal conflicts have to do with triangular relationships, with the feelings that get stirred up in the interaction between three people – three friends in a playground, a husband, wife, and lover, a child and his two parents, a husband, wife, and mother-in-law, for example. This can be an arena in which powerful feelings of being included, excluded, being in competition with, having loving and hateful feelings towards others, get played out. The therapist might step into this arena even at the first session. We have spoken earlier about how therapy can fail at the very beginning because the patient finds that loyalty to his partner or parent will not allow him to include the therapist as a significant other in his life. Because at some stage he was not able to move from relating to one other important person to being able to relate to more than one person at a time, he might get into difficulty in making a commitment to therapy. He might be literally faced with a choice between his wife and his therapist. Finding himself in an untenable situation with both wife and therapist, he must extract himself from one. He feels he has a choice to have one, but not to have both.

In this situation the therapist will at times have to allow the therapy to finish prematurely. At other times, the patient will have the capacity to consider the conflicting loyalties that he is experiencing. Knowing that the therapist understands his dilemma, and experiencing over time that she does not pressure him to go further into his feelings than he can manage, might allow him to continue until he is more able to cope with the inevitable conflict. Occasionally, a patient feels under so much pressure that understanding on the part of the therapist is not sufficient. He might, for instance, need to cut down his session time as the only way short of stopping completely to allay his overbearing guilt about disloyalty to his partner. In time, as he works less intensely, he might be able to use the additional session again. A similar pattern can happen in relation, not to another person, but to a place or a position such as a new home, job, or outside interest.

The place of the third person in the triangle is taken by this loyalty and he is again in conflict, needing to pursue one or the other, but not both.

'*I no longer have symptoms so I no longer need to come here*'

One of Jung's innovations was to look at symptoms in a new way. He saw them not as something to be eliminated, but as a means of drawing attention to a hitherto unnoticed aspect of the patient's personality – as if he were saying to himself and others, 'This is where I am hurting.' Jung developed his form of treatment partly in response to the bizarre behaviour of psychotic patients. He took exception to the label 'irrational' and, as he so often did, turned it on its head, wondering what the symptom might be communicating that was actually quite 'rational'. In other words, symptoms were seen as a form of symbolic language that needed to be deciphered according to an inner system of logic. Although we are not discussing work with patients in psychotic states, Jung's approach has been used by modern-day Jungians in the consulting room to consider what the symptom means. It is not considered an irrational language, rather an unknown or forgotten one. Part of its purpose is to draw our attention to something that we might otherwise ignore.

Viewed from this angle, the symptom that disappears soon after therapy commences has already served an important function. It has mobilized the patient, and maybe those around him, to take action. It has alerted the therapist. We can assume that some relief is being experienced. The patient is in a place of safety and concern and might not need this particular means of communication any longer because he has heard and we are alerted. But a symptom disappearing is not the same as being in good health or no longer needing help. It is almost as if the symptom has done its part of the job in getting the therapy established and now expects the interaction between patient and therapist to take over. On many occasions this is exactly what happens. Having been alerted to a problem, the patient is able to use the therapeutic experience to begin to look at his own previously neglected conflicts and feelings.

In other instances, it is much less straightforward. The patient has gained some relief, maybe even in the first session. But his thinking is concrete. If the wound can no longer be seen, why go to the doctor for further bandages? He finds it hard to believe that there might be more, longer term, wounding inside that cannot be seen so easily. Sometimes, he will resist any suggestion along these lines and will have to stop prematurely until perhaps another symptom brings him back to the therapist or someone else. Over time, a series of mishaps might be the only thing to convince him of his underlying need. Very often, people come to therapy at a time when they begin to see a pattern of happenings in their lives, when they can no longer explain them away as separate, random events.

'*I think this is really a physical problem that needs medical attention*'

Sometimes this statement is made explicitly. At other times the patient simply gets ill, sometimes to such an extent that he can no longer come to therapy. Remember that we are looking in this section at ways of ending prematurely. Illness can be used in this manner, but not all illness is therefore defensive. Again we are talking about the meaning and intent behind the illness, not the illness *per se*. It is important that physical problems are investigated medically in their own right, particularly as we have become aware of the complexity of the interaction between mind and body. It seems probable that feelings can cause illness through their interaction with hormones. On the other hand, there is little doubt that physical problems cause stress and that the two also interact in ways we do not yet understand.

Clinical example

A patient comes to therapy with every intention of using the sessions to explore his unhappiness. But somehow the words and understanding of the counsellor do not reach him. He is looking for the 'hands on', practical kind of comfort that a medical practitioner might be able to offer. When he has a physical problem in the course of therapy he yearns for this kind of direct care and feels that in choosing to come to therapy he has made a mistake. He suggests stopping therapy and consulting a medical specialist. It is not surprising that his father was a doctor and that only through physical care at times of illness could he communicate his love and affection for his son.

Physical symptoms are concrete and for many patients less frightening than emotional ones. They do not carry the same overtone of blame, shame, connection to mental illness or, at worst, madness. Often they can be put right more immediately, with the secondary gain of physical care and comfort, and there might be a greater expectation that the pain will not go on forever.

Protecting the therapist

In the above paragraphs we have suggested a number of ways in which the therapy might come to an impasse.

There is another factor that might operate, one that is often concealed behind more obvious reasons, both from the therapist and, sometimes, from the patient himself. The therapy might get stuck. The therapist might come under strong pressure to stop because there are powerful unresolved feelings towards the therapist that threaten to break through into consciousness and from which there is an equally strong need to protect both therapist and patient. It might be that other negative feelings can and have been expressed in the course of the work, but acknowledging dissatisfaction with someone who is apparently trying to help might be one step too far. This can be the case when it is not a specific thing that has been upsetting, but a more general feeling of not getting on, of the therapist not being right. It can also be the case when strong erotic or aggressive feelings so disturb the patient that he would rather end the therapy than reveal them. It is as if there is a terrible secret that cannot be told.

Clinical example

There are times when a particular match of patient and therapist does not seem to work. In some instances a patient might move on to work more successfully with another person. On the other hand, a patient might have grown up feeling that he was in the wrong family, but unable to put it right or to say anything for fear of hurting his parents. This is an example of someone who produced all sorts of practical reasons why it was reasonable to stop therapy, and as soon as possible, before the power of his negative feelings became too great to hold back. One day the therapist said, 'Something just isn't right.' The patient – a usually controlled young man – burst into tears. With relief, he could finally admit that things weren't right. He didn't feel they got on because he had so many secret dissatisfactions with the therapist. This 'letting go' of feelings and of the shame that surrounded them enabled the therapy to become unstuck and eventually to continue.

'*Do you want me to stay?*'

Any of the above examples of premature ending could be used by the patient as a means of discovering whether the therapist wants him enough to struggle to keep him. Does the therapist care enough in a personal way to go to some effort to hold on to him? After all, the prospect of leaving brings up the immediate relationship between patient and therapist, and if it is felt to be premature it can challenge the therapist's judgement in a very personal manner. Despite the therapist maintaining a neutral stance, a patient might become aware that his leaving in such a manner *does* matter to the therapist and therefore *he* matters. This reassurance might enable him to continue.

The effect on the therapist

The attempt to stop or end prematurely can be experienced by the therapist as, and often is, an attack on the therapeutic work. It might be an unconscious attack and therefore one that the patient has little control over. But whatever the particular dynamics, it is likely to have an effect on the therapist. In some of our examples, the encounter led to a breakthrough and the recognition of difficult and previously unexpressed feelings that in turn allowed the therapy to progress. In other cases, the therapy had to end, at least for the time being, despite the ending being in the therapist's judgement premature.

However, the patient is only one part of the equation. The therapist is the other, and the process of dealing with the intention to stop prematurely and of having to face a premature end can take its toll. For one reason or another, the patient does not want to continue. We can understand this in many of the ways outlined above, but it can also be experienced as a personal attack (which on some occasions it is!). There is something about this particular kind of attempt by the patient that invariably seems to 'fit' with the therapist's uncertainties about her own work. The combination can make it virtually impossible to know whether or not one is at this moment competent and can raise anxieties that the patient, in his desire to leave, is probably right to do so. The therapist begins to feel that she is indeed the bad therapist, not unlike the patient's bad mother. Just at a time that she needs her stability, she may become anxious and unsure. This is a time when supervision is crucial. The patient can so undermine the therapist she does 'become' the bad mother and does not know how to cope. Outside reflection can restore her equilibrium (good maternal instincts) and save the therapy. Also the knowledge that what the patient is doing to the therapist is probably what was done to him in the past – feeling thoroughly bad because of being rejected – can help.

The task or purpose of an ending

We have taken a long time to get to one of the central issues of ending. Let us assume that an ending happens, *not* prematurely, but in a 'good-enough' fashion. What is the task or purpose of this phase of the work? It is a truism to say that each ending will be unique, and we do not have space to go into the many individual variations. However, there are certain ingredients common to an ending. In the most general terms, it is a time to remember the past, to reflect on the time spent together, and to anticipate the future. More precisely, it will involve some or all of the following processes.

Looking at change

The approaching end is likely to throw into relief what has happened since the beginning of the work. This will, in turn, highlight what change or development has taken place. Naturally, there will be a difference between the end of a short-term counselling or psychotherapy contract and several years of more intensive psychotherapy. Nevertheless, even a few sessions, or indeed a single session, can have an ending phase and the possibility of change within that time. The young mother we spoke of earlier, uncertain about whether or not to keep her baby, might have come to an important, though painful decision within a few sessions. To do this, she will have had to face what she could not face when she first approached the counsellor – the feelings of rejection towards the baby that she was keeping hidden from herself because of the strong reaction of her mother. Despite the short-term nature of this piece of work, the counsellor gave her space – unlike her mother – to acknowledge her other feelings and so to come to a decision.

Sometimes, change is obvious to both client and counsellor. At other times, it will be apparent only to the practitioner. For some of the people who seek help, change of any kind might be an unfamiliar state or, if it does occur, it might be rarely talked about. In such cases, the counsellor will need to take the lead and point out what might be obvious to her, but have been largely unnoticed by the client himself.

Making a space for gratitude and thanks

It will depend on the patient's openness and on the nature of the relationship with the counsellor whether and to what extent the changes that have occurred can be acknowledged and whether there can be mutual pleasure in what has happened in the work together. When it is possible for such feelings to be openly recognized, then it might be possible for the client to know about and express gratitude or thanks for the time together and for the change that has occurred. Some people will have the words to express this; for others, finding such words might be a new and important aspect of the work during this ending phase. Many people come to therapeutic work with little or no experience of having been thanked or recognized themselves, or of expressing such appreciation to someone else. Silence might not mean they do not feel appreciative but simply that they have not heard such words used about themselves or know how to use them about others. Helping such a person find, use, and experience the words might be an invaluable part of the ending experience. Other people will express such feelings concretely through gifts, tears, or perhaps a cautious smile. When unexpected, the counsellor can feel caught off guard. Some thinking or reflection about the process beforehand might help to contain a sense of embarrassment or awkwardness. There are times such as these when it is helpful to the client for the counsellor to be able to respond on an ordinary social level.

Acknowledging what has happened

In contrast to what might have changed in the work, there will also be expectations that have not been met, the inevitable disappointments. It is, of course, just as important to have space to express such feelings as it is for those of appreciation. Again, this will depend on the relationship between therapist and client and on the client's capacity for self-reflection. It will also depend on the therapist's own openness and the extent to which she can tolerate hearing what might be said. Having space to acknowledge what has not happened can, paradoxically, allow it to start happening. Facing this kind of disappointment or anger with a significant person might be a part of what did not happen in the past and until now has not happened between therapist and client.

Acknowledging what has not happened is important for other reasons. It can set the stage for the future–for what the client might want to return to later on, what he might be able to continue with on his own, or sometimes what he decides at the eleventh hour to continue with in his present therapy. Of course, it is possible that what was not done could not have been done given the situation the client was in or the limitations on time (which he might have curtailed so it could not happen). However, it is still important to recognize *the expectations* that were not met. It might even be possible to acknowledge, with the wisdom of hindsight, what part the client himself played in the way the work evolved.

Feelings about ending

An important aspect of the ending is having time and space to have feelings about the relationship finishing. The relationship has occurred within the boundaries of a professional contract, but for both parties involved it will usually have had a personal element. Inevitably there will be feelings about the relationship ending, and this can be the case even when the contact has been difficult, little has happened, or when the desire to end has been a preoccupation from the very beginning.

Acknowledging loss is like any other kind of mourning in that it is one way of helping to deal with, and eventually to mitigate, the pain. When it is left undone or cannot be done, it can be difficult for both client and therapist. For the client, it can mean being left with unexpressed feelings that can affect his future equilibrium in a variety of ways. In some cases, it can be the unconscious motivation behind the client's attempts to remain in touch afterwards, by phoning, writing letters, calling in on the therapist, attempting to meet in public, or otherwise intruding on her privacy.

Likewise, there are dangers for the counsellor of not acknowledging to himself or perhaps a supervisor what the ending has meant. When there is no space for this kind of reflection, the counsellor, like the patient, can 'act it out' unconsciously. This can take the form of 'living off one's work' or of using a new patient to fill the emotional space left by another, thereby not allowing the new patient to have his own space. Although the relationship between counsellor and patient is not reciprocal, it will have a meaning for both. It is important for each to have a space to recognize that meaning so as to prevent its enactment.

After the ending

In the foregoing discussion we have been focusing on what it is possible to explore with the client during the ending phase of the work. Because the end *is* the end, and in addition might reveal previously unrecognized feelings (which could take both client and counsellor by surprise), there will inevitably be reactions after the ending when the work of reflection continues alone or with a supervisor. In the ideal situation, enough has gone on in the work together for the client to internalize helpful aspects of his counsellor or psychotherapist which then becomes the basis for an independent existence afterwards. Apart from the practical changes that might have occurred, it is to be hoped that there will have been a change in self-awareness or in how the client thinks about himself.

Summary and conclusion

How does one end – or draw a boundary around – our discussion on boundaries? The common theme in all of the chapters has been the central and, indeed, defining role of boundaries and containment in psychodynamic work, whether in short- or long-term counselling or in any of the various forms of psychotherapy. Looking at the function of boundaries and containment in the larger world outside therapeutic work, it is not an exaggeration to say that what is inside the containing perimeter is, to some extent, defined by the nature of the outside boundary.

When we look at a landscape, our eyes are drawn to the defining edges of the fields – the hedgerows, the stone walls, the farm gates, the stiles and fences that form the boundaries. Although they are not the only aspect of the landscape or of what happens within their perimeter, they do have a powerful influence on what happens inside. For instance, as some of the traditional boundaries of the landscape, the hedgerows, have been eliminated to allow the farmer greater scope and ease in planting his crops, the quality of the space within has changed for the wildlife that depends on the hedgerow edges of fields to survive. Likewise, stone walls that have been allowed to deteriorate determine the nature of the livestock that can be kept inside. Whether you identify with the wildlife or with the farmer, boundaries and the effect of what happens at and within them are vital.

Another theme that has been implicit in the book is that interaction very often happens at boundaries. This is true in the psychotherapeutic world as well as in the world beyond. Consider neighbours chatting or, indeed, fighting over the garden fence. Consider wars, both national and civil, over defining, indeed defending, inside space from outside space. Here, the exact placement of a boundary becomes something for which some would literally kill or be killed. Consider celebrations and anniversaries at the beginning or end of a new space. It is at this boundary between the old and the new that we stop to acknowledge the importance of what has happened within the perimeter of the old space, perhaps the first twenty-five years of a marriage, or to consider what will happen at the beginning of the new space, perhaps, for the student, the beginning of university, or, for a country, the installation of a new leader.

Indeed, it is often at such times that people decide to come into therapy in the first place. It is in the nature of boundaries that they have a defining function. Therefore, they can bring into focus issues that until then have remained hidden. For example, a hard working executive maintains an impossibly demanding work schedule until he has a heart attack. How often do we hear later that this was the defining moment of his life—the point at which he could no longer ignore the pleas of doctor, family, and friends, maybe even himself. In a dramatic manner, the heart attack draws an immediate boundary around his work. It says, 'You are stopping now. This is the limit.' As we review the preceding period of time, the time before the attack, the first twenty-five years of a marriage, or years of work at the time of retirement, patterns are thrown into relief. It is not surprising that these times are often called 'turning points', times at which decisions are made to alter direction or to face what could not be seen while in the middle of the experience. Thus, boundaries have the capacity to make us question fundamental aspects of our lives.

It is not accidental that this sort of 'stock-taking' so often happens at boundaries. When we mourn and celebrate the end of a life at the funeral, we are in large part considering the meaning of that life to us. We are stopping at a boundary and taking time to acknowledge what has been before. In a much more trivial way, when we stop to climb over a stile or negotiate a farm fence, we pause and might notice the landscape that we have just walked over or that we are about to tackle. So, boundaries and the containment defined by them provide a setting in which to see patterns, to evaluate, to consider, to change direction, and, most importantly, to confer meaning. It is all of this that we are doing in and through our therapeutic work.

Perhaps the ultimate question we might ask about the use of boundaries and containment in our work is this: to what extent does the person in therapy or counselling feel safely contained? Is it sufficient to facilitate the things that might be involved in that encounter – the exploring, the expression of thought and feeling, and the self-reflection?

For, in the end, we are attempting to provide a space in which the person can begin to establish the trust necessary for the work to happen.

REFERENCES

Access to Health Records Act (1990). London: HMSO.

Anzieu, D. (1989). *The Skin Ego*. New Haven, CT: Yale University Press.

Bion, W. R. (1988). *Attention and Interpretation*. London: Karnac.

Bollas, C. (2003). Confidentiality and professionalism in psychoanalysis. *British Journal of Psychotherapy*, *20*: 157–176.

British Confederation of Psychotherapists' Working Group on Confidentiality (2003). BCP introductory statement on confidentiality. *British Journal of Psychotherapy*, *20*: 191–194.

Britton, R. (1989). The missing link: parental sexuality in the Oedipus complex. In: J. Steiner (Ed.), *The Oedipus Complex Today* (pp. 83–101). London: Karnac.

Children Act (1989). London: HMSO

Data Protection Act (1998). London: HMSO.

Fordham, M. (1985). *Explorations into the Self*. London: LAP/Academic Press.

Freud, S. (1905e). Fragment of an analysis of a case of hysteria ('Dora'), *S.E.*, *7*: 1–22. London: Hogarth

Freud, S. (1912b). The dynamics of transference, *S.E.*, *12*. London: Hogarth.

Freud, S. (1915). The unconscious. *S.E.*, *14*: 159–215. London: Hogarth.

Freud, S. (1940a). An outline of psycho-analysis. *S.E.*, *23*: 141-208. London: Hogarth.

Freud, S., & Breuer, J. (1895d). Case history 2: Frau Emmy von N. *S.E.*, *2*: 48–105. London: Hogarth.

Gabbard, G. O., & Lester, E. P. (1995). *Boundaries and Boundary Violations in Psychoanalysis*. New York: Basic Books.

Human Rights Act (1998). London: HMSO.

Jung, C. G. (1931a). Problems of modern psychotherapy. In: *The Practice of Psychotherapy, C.W., 16*: para. 114–174. London: Routledge & Kegan Paul.

Jung, C. G. (1931b). Marriage as a psychological relationship. In: *The Development of Personality, C.W., 17*: para. 324–345. London: Routledge & Kegan Paul.

Jung, C. G. (1935). Principles of practical psychotherapy. In: *The Practice of Psychotherapy, C.W., 16*: para, 1–27. London: Routledge & Kegan Paul.

Jung, C. G. (1946). Specific problems of psychotherapy III: The psychology of the transference. In: *The Practice of Psychotherapy, C.W., 16*: para. 353–401. London: Routledge & Kegan Paul.

Jung, C. G. (1952). Synchronicity: an acausal connecting principle. In: *The Structures and Dynamics of the Psyche, C.W., 8:* para. 816–968. London: Routledge & Kegan Paul.

Jung, C. G. (1953). The spirit mercurius. In: *Alchemical Studies, C.W.*, 13: para. 239–303. London: Routledge & Kegan Paul.

Jung, C. G. (1958). The transcendent function. In: *The Structures and Dynamics of the Psyche, C.W.*, 8: para. 131–193. London: Routledge & Kegan Paul.

Karpf, A. (1999). My weeping skin: crying without tears. In: *Journal of the British Association of Psychotherapists, 36*: 3–14.

Klein, M. (1946). Notes on some schizoid mechanisms. In: *Envy and Gratitude, and Other Works, 1946–1963.* London: Hogarth.

Layton, A. (2003). Setting the scene III: The perspective of a sympathetic outsider. *British Journal of Psychotherapy, 20*: 149–156.

Lucas, R. (2002). Report on Conference. *APP Newsletter, 27.*

Mennella, J. (2005). Monell Institute of Philadelphia As reported in the Independent Newspaper, John Von Radowitz, 28 November 2005.

Menzies Lyth, I. (1988). *Containing Anxiety in Institutions: Selected Essays, Vol. 1.* London: Free Association.

Sandler, A.-M. (2004). Institutional responses to boundary violations. *International Journal of Psychoanalysis, 85*:27–43.

Winnicott, D. W. (1985). The capacity for concern In: *The Maturational Processes and the Facilitating Environment.* London: Hogarth.

INDEX

Printed in Great Britain
by Amazon